Each building block has its primary function to create an income, its secondary function is then to refer business to other building blocks and receive business to supplement its own growth.

Layne Lancefield and Staci Chamberlain are the authors of '5 passive income streams in five days' and '50 ways that people make extra money for additional income'. Built on the success of their previous books, 'Compounding Income' builds on the principle of online income that feeds and refers to your other online passive income streams to create a compounding (or in simple terms, a snowballing) effect that is multiplied by the power of the number of streams both feeding and being fed. If you have read '5 Income Steams in Five days', you'll understand Layne and Staci's devotion to the idea of *Under Promise and Over Deliver* where they taught many more than five income streams and **Compounding Income** will deliver many more than 10 income streams by the time you're finished.

Each of these income streams can stand on their own but with links to each other they become powerful. Even if you decide not to use all of them, study them anyway because it's likely they will prompt you with ideas to use elsewhere.

Instead of a contents page that fast forwards you to certain sections, we recommend that you read through this how to guide form start to finish with a highlighter marking the pages that grab your attention. You'll find that some income streams are 'mechanical' meaning you simply follow what we do and it will produce results but if you're prepared to be creative and produce material that is interesting, entertaining, helpful and useful, then you will absolutely excel!
Everybody is good at something and you'll soon see that people are very happy to pay a fair price for that knowledge, for those ideas, for that entertainment and for that assistance.

What differentiates the COMPOUNDING INCOME model from other forms of on-line income is that it is truly passive. There are many ways to make an income online but most methods end up being a second job instead of creating passive, ongoing income.

Remember, the biggest battle is always in the mind! It's about staying positive with a can-do attitude and working through the exercises. If you are completely new, you might be best to plan the implementation of what you learn over more than ten days, remember, you will learn how to create many more than just ten income streams so take your time to understand and you'll be rewarded with the income that you desire.

Layne took three years to learn and implement what you will learn in under two weeks. Layne made his first dollar on-line using Create Space back in 2008 and by 2011 he was generating enough income on-line to replace what his wife was earning. Layne now works a couple of hours a week adding to his online income streams.

The effort you put in will determine the outcome (or better income) that you derive from what you learn. This book will only be of value if you implement what you learn and overcome those who will try and tell you that it can't be done. Layne says the biggest hurdle to generating an online income was overcoming the negativity from other people, he said working through the *"it can't be done people"* was more work that actually building the online streams so before you even start, make up your mind that you will succeed and this will be more than you ever hoped for.

Enjoy!

Online Income
The Ultimate Guide to Create Online Income Streams

Whether you're an absolute beginner with zero programing skills or you already have knowledge of on-line income and you want to expand, then this book is for you.

This will be the most exciting guide you have ever read, why? Because it will teach you exactly how to build your first ten income streams and then build the links that feed each other to increase your income. With each link being both a source of business and a referrer of business, the net effect of this Cross Collateralization is a Compounding Income and a business model where you only work on the business and never in it.

This book has three important categories;
1. The theory- a behind the scenes look at online income
2. The method – a step-by-step how-to guide including the websites that you'll need.
3. Actual ideas to help you along.

To be truly passive, the COMPOUNDING INCOME method builds the business of on-line income without ongoing work. It's a methodology where you don't mind putting in the work to start the business as long as you earn money from that business on an ongoing basis. The business that generated that money then refers buyers and thereby income to other legs of your on-line model that also refer business back, thereby creating an effective compounding income with zero risk and in most cases zero outlay.

This self-sustaining on-line business model has no need for programing skills, employees or ongoing money to be spent supporting it. What it does require is a desire to succeed, an ability to hold onto a vision and the dedication to put time and effort into learning new ways of doing things.

This book is an absolute step by step guide but you will still need to put in the time to learn so our recommendation is that you read through this book in full before you even sit at your computer, that way you'll have a great understanding of the overall concept of on-line income from multiple streams. You'll understand how to manage the various systems and programs that we will use, you'll understand why we link our projects and you'll see from the outset that the time you are about to put in will truly pay you a sustainable, reliable, ongoing income.

The first layer of this book is a step by step guide for both beginners who have never built an on-line income as well as those more experienced to build new income streams. This first stage deals with the foundation, the building blocks that on their own will generate a passive and ongoing income.

The next stage is to leverage off these building blocks to create 'spin-off' income. This is income that is not directly related to that particular business but is complementary to that income 'building block'.

The third stage is to link all of these building blocks together in the same way that the veins in your body link all your muscles together by supplying oxygen rich blood to create a system that works in harmony.

Stage One

Let's start by outlining the methods we'll use to generate an income by grouping them into three basic categories;

The first is ***proprietary***, in other works your own work. If you have a hobby, a skill, a particular knowledge or understanding then you can sell it.
The second category is ***affiliated income***, in other words a commission from business that you refer for a third party.
The third category is ***advertising***, in other words a payment that you receive in return for running an ad on behalf of somebody else.

 **Success Tip!**

If you don't understand something, keep reading and come back to it later because we will cover things in more detail as we go.

The highest income will usually come from what you put the most amount of time into. At the low end of the scale, this is perfecting the grouping of advertisements, at the mid stage it is the methods we use referring business and at the top end of the scale it is original work that you produce.

If you have ever considered being an author and producing books, CD's, DVDs, music, fiction or how-to manuals, then this is your time to shine!

If you enjoy helping people understand a subject, fix something or teach then you can sell that knowledge. If you can make music, if you can inspire or if you pass on knowledge then you can create an ongoing income that once you have produced, it will generate an ongoing income with zero further input.

For this stage, the best place to start is the Create Space website. This is a sister site to Amazon where you can create your own books, CDs, DVDs and MP3s that can then be sold to the whole world on Amazon. There is no cost and this is a great place to start. Let's log onto **www.createspace.com** and open an account. This will be the first of dozens of accounts that we will open so we suggest that you use a spread sheet to record all your passwords such as Excel.

For the example we will upload this book you are reading, Compounding Income.

Once this is done we can also upload it to **Kindle** and you will have created your first two online income streams.

The Links to your Create Space page can be used in emails, blogs, websites and just about any digital media to promote your own material.

This will lead onto other self-publishing websites that we'll cover later but we have found Create Space to be the easiest place to start. From here you can produce a professional physical book (for free!) and you can then load it onto Kindle as an eBook.

As with any book you'll need to invest time, care and a passion to produce content that is valuable. Layne produced his first book back in 2008 by interviewing dozens of people from the same culture about their success in business and Staci's first books were fiction.

Their sales increased greatly with the first edition of "50 Ways that People Make Extra Money for Additional Income". It was a simple book with 50 examples of how people made additional income and what made it easy to produce was the fact they simply interviewed people whom they met through work.

Layne and Staci began interviewing people from particular business such as financial planning and recording the interview. They made a list of thirty five questions to ask and then asked people for an interview, they would email the list of thirty five questions and ask their 'client' to pick twenty that they were comfortable answering such as methods used to grow their business.

This gave Layne and Staci content to publish in both physical print and on CD (and MP3). Before leaving the interview, they asked their client for referrals to other people who would be happy to be interviewed for their business program. Layne and Staci edited each interview to twenty questions in twenty minutes and put three sessions to each CD. The Create Space website provides a link that can be used in emails, blogs and just about any other digital media to promote their CD. One Financial Planner, while being interviewed explained that most planners work through an aggregator who provides access to a wider range of products and financial institutions. With this knowledge they began contacting aggregators who then paid them to advertise on their CDs. The aggregators also promoted the CDs through their emails and newsletters.

Layne and Staci got this idea while interviewing a pilot for their book '50 ways that people make extra money for additional income'. This pilot had made DVDs to help with lessons and he was selling them in his newsletter and emails through his Create Space account. He would suggest his students buy the DVD in advance of their next lesson, he said his DVDs were not cheap but they were far cheaper than a lesson in a helicopter!

While interviewing people for the same book, they met Hayden, a fireman who sells books on Amazon (through Create Space) with advice for people wanting to join the fire brigade. Hayden is a great example of somebody using their knowledge to make an online income. How-to guides are probably the easiest to produce if you have knowledge in that area.

For example, you can produce a book or DVD on laying bricks, pavers or tiling if that's what you're good at. You can produce material on parenting, babysitting or cleaning if that's what you enjoy. If you're into horses you could produce a book or DVD on the top ten tips from the top equestrian people that you know. The same can be said of Golfers, Fishing experts and just about any other hobby or skill.

The main point to remember is that it has to be informative, entertaining or helpful. In other words it must be value for money. People will pay for your material as long as it represents value for what they paid.

Another idea is using material that it in the public domain. Some people frown on this idea but plenty of people make money from it.

Try **www.gutenberg.org/** or search the Wikipedia Public Domain page **http://en.wikipedia.org/wiki/Wikipedia:Public_domain_image_resources** (or just Google Public Domain)

To test this theory, we found a free copy of "Acres of Diamonds" by Russell Conwell and uploaded it on our Create Space account to sell on Amazon. There were many other copies available and the cheapest was fifty cents more than the minimum price set by Create Space. As a proof of concept we set the price at twenty cents above our minimum price and sold thirty nine copies in two weeks. On one hand we didn't make much money ($7.80) but on the other hand we proved that it was a viable concept. It's worth noting that when we tried to upload it to **Kindle** it was rejected.

Another way you can produce material is by outsourcing your requirements. For four years we have used "Get Friday" (www.getfriday.com) to source everything from data bases to blog content. They are based in India and will usually get the information back to you the next day. We pay a flat fee of $15 a month and then $15 an hour when we give them a project.

If you decide to give them a go, we suggest you manage them the same way you would any other employee, in other words don't just give them 'free rein' but set goals and time frames for them.
For example, we would say please research idea X for a maximum of one hour by this time tomorrow and provide X amount of information.
If you Google 'Get Friday' you'll find more outsourcing companies. You could also use Fivver (**http://fiverr.com**) to find people who will be happy to write content, build websites and source material from $5.

The place not to create material, at least not the creative stuff is your office or lounge room because there are too many distractions. Try going for a walk with a notepad and pen, somewhere that there are no distractions such as the beach, your favorite river or the hills. When you're quiet and alone with your notepad you'll be able to concentrate and create an outline of your material.

While researching for the book '50 ways that people make extra money for additional income' Staci met Karen and Cheryl who used and recommended "Appster" to make iPhone and Android Apps. They had bought books and tried to learn 'X Code' (The code used to program iPhone apps) but were disappointed in the amount of time needed to learn a new language so outsourcing to Appster (**http://www.appster.com.au/**) allowed them to create the income from their idea with wasting time learning code. Of course this cost them money to produce but for them it was a great investment.

If you decide to produce a book, the easiest method is to type that content into a word document and save it as a PDF. You can then upload that PDF directly to the Create Space website.

We'll cover other Print on Demand websites such Lighting Source (**http://www1.lightningsource.com**) and LuLu (**www.LuLu.com**) later.

We suggest you start with Create Space because you can then easily sell on Amazon and Kindle.
Let's run through a simple example of uploading this book.
Go to **www.createspace.com** and open a new account.

You can load your book to both LuLu and Create Space if you wish, they'll even both create a free ISBN for you. (book tracking number)

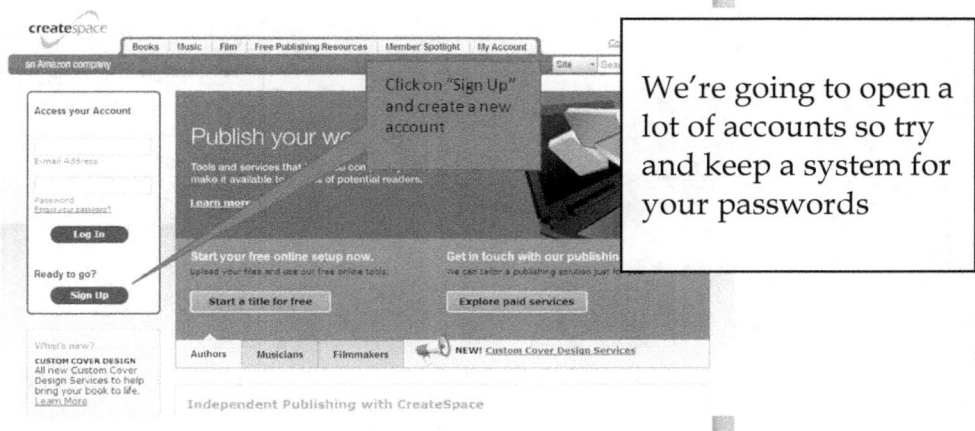

We're going to open a lot of accounts so try and keep a system for your passwords

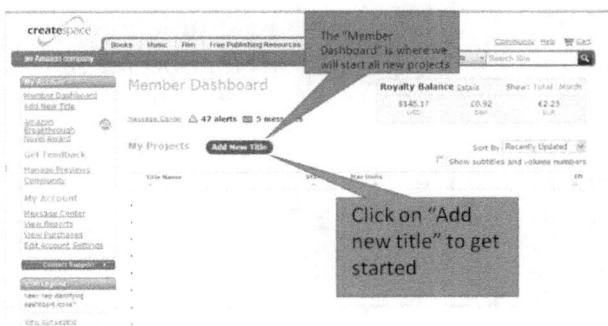

Once you've signed up, you'll be directed to the "Member Dashboard" This is where we'll start new projects

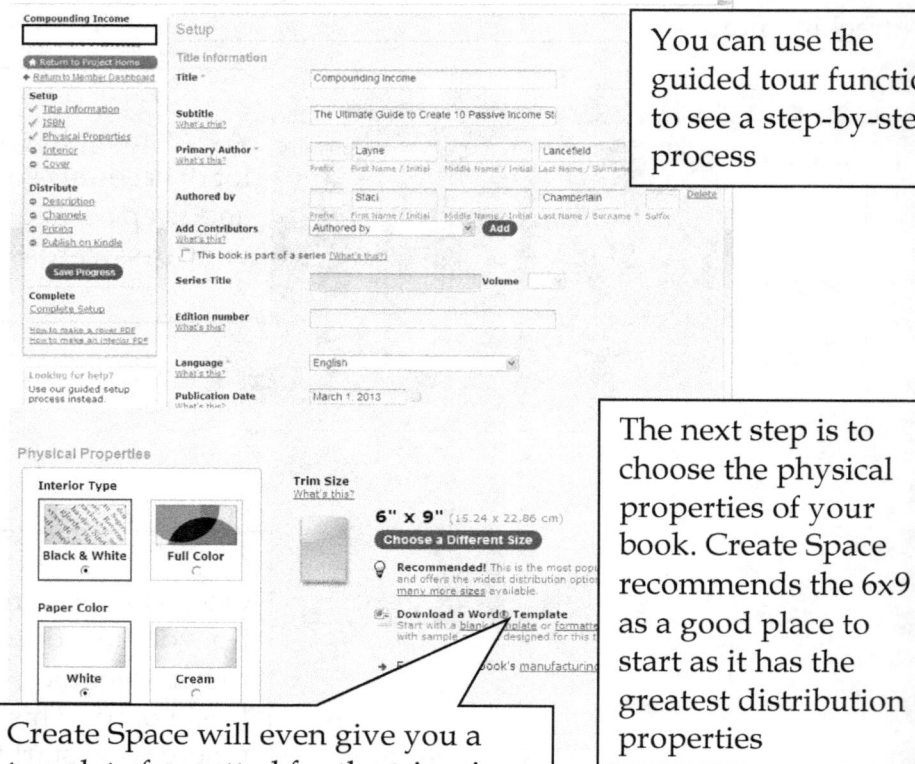

You can use the guided tour functio to see a step-by-step process

The next step is to choose the physical properties of your book. Create Space recommends the 6x9 as a good place to start as it has the greatest distribution properties

Create Space will even give you a template formatted for the trim size that you choose.

The next step is to upload the interior file. The interior file needs to be in PDF format. If you don't have a PDF converter you can visit the Adobe website and convert up to five files for free

Next, launch the cover creator…

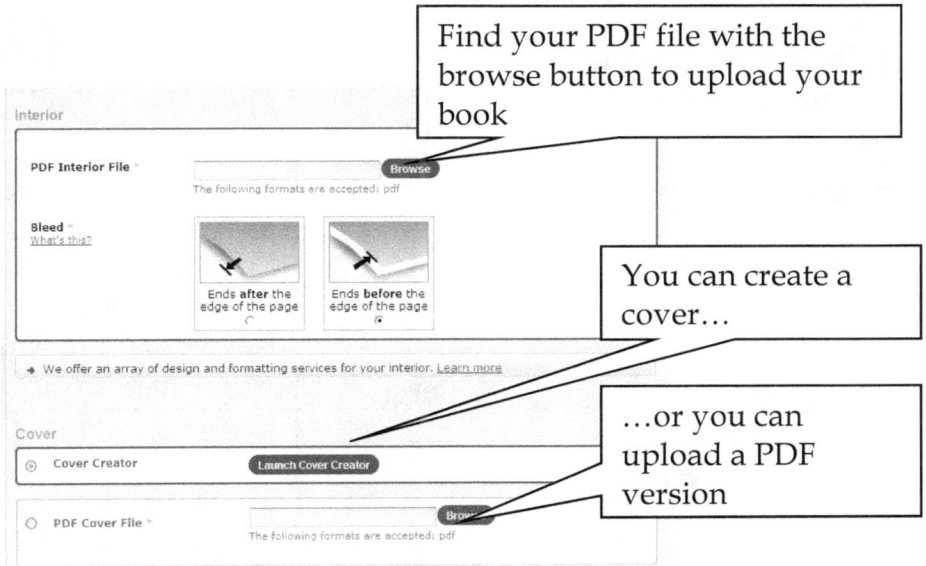

Find your PDF file with the browse button to upload your book

You can create a cover…

…or you can upload a PDF version

The Cover Creator is easy to use, simply follow the steps to choose the template that you want. You can then change the background colours, the font and what details are displayed such as an authors photo. You can upload your own cover photo or use one supplied by Create Space.

You can also make your own cover and upload it as a PDF.

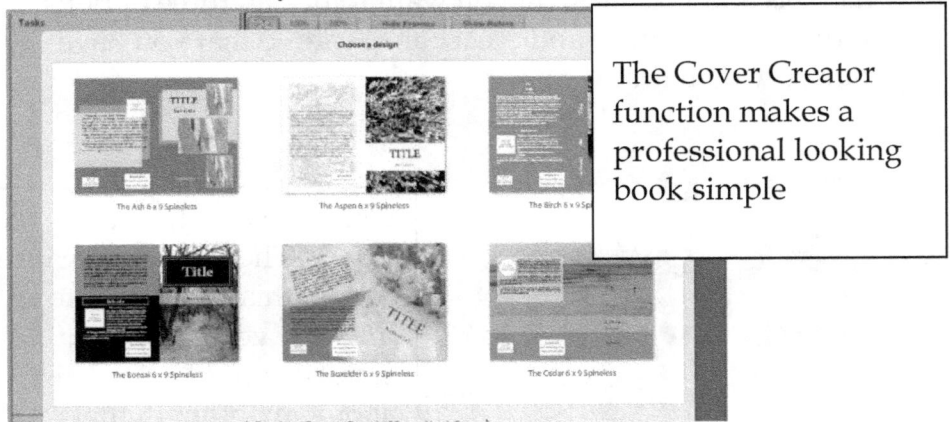

The Cover Creator function makes a professional looking book simple

The key words you use in your description will help it be found

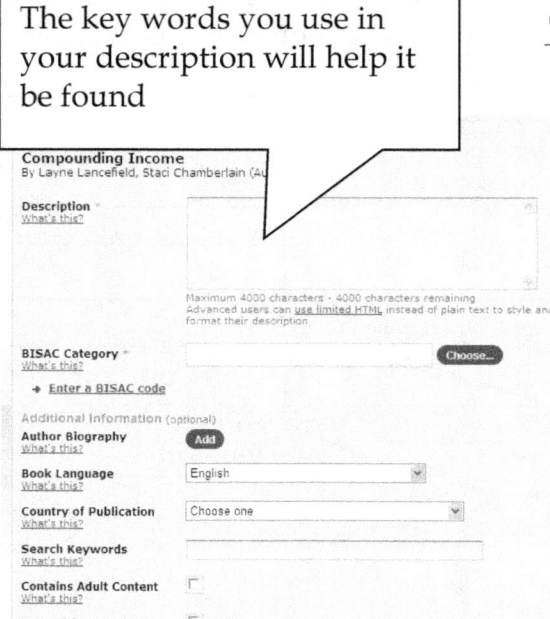

These next few steps are very important. The "description" field and "Search Keywords" are what will help sell your book.

The description needs to be an accurate, brief and compelling outline of your book.

The key search words box allows you to use five words that people would search Amazon to find your book. The best words to use would discribe both your book and it's title.

As you move through each step you will come to distribution, channels and Pricing. You will want to tick all three options on the channels page and create an eStore so that you have your very own link.

Select the CreateSpace eStore. Then click on 'eStore set up' this will generate a link that you can use in emails, your blog and just about any other digital media to help promote your book!

Finally, you can press the "Submit for Review" button and Create Space will review your files. They look for things such as the 'bleed' meaning the text does not go off the page, they check to make sure any pictures are resonable quality and that the book is up to standard. The approval process is usually done within 24 hours and your on the way to making money online as a self-published author!

Once your book is approved and you have reviewed it , either by ordering a physical copy or reviewing a digital copy, you can then approve it for world wide publication.

When you have approved your book, you'll be given the option to load the files onto the Kindle system. This is another reason we chose to use Create Space as the program will also create an eBook for you.

You don't even have to convert the files, it'll do it all for you. Simply click on "publish to Kindle" and then "manage my book on KDP" (Kindle Direct Publishing)

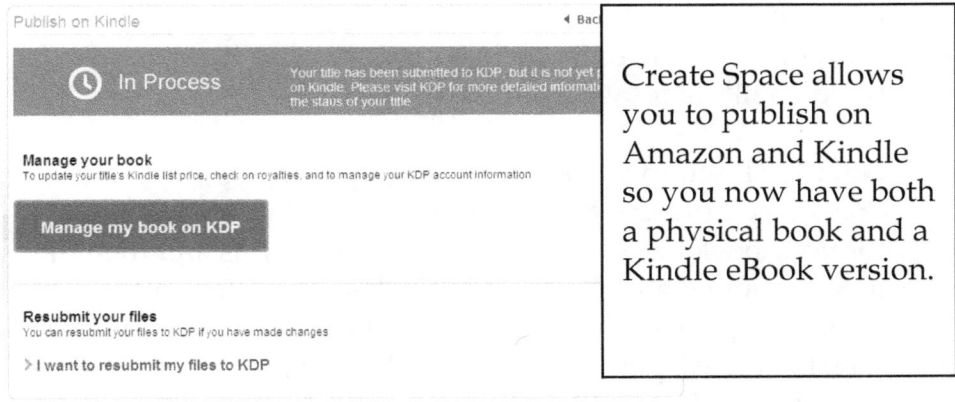

Create Space allows you to publish on Amazon and Kindle so you now have both a physical book and a Kindle eBook version.

There are a couple of very important points to take note of here.
First, congratulations on having just published a book.
Second, you now have two income streams, Amazon and Kindle.
Third, you also have a link that will take people to your own eStore where they will only see your book. You can use this link in emails, on your blog or even publish it in physical newsletters and printed articals.

If you were to stop here and do nothing more you would make maoney online for years to come without doing another thing.

You might also consider some of the other options of On-Demand-Printing such as Lighting Source and LuLu.

Before we move on to other income streams we need to consider methods of promoting what you have just created. We'll cover this process in more detail later but to understand the compounding income methodology we'll touch on some of the methods.
The book or DVD that you just prodcued has it's own search words built in but we want more than that.

Later we'll set up a blog using Google's Blogger (or Word Press if you prefer). From this blog we will publish a 'teaser' for your book or DVD with a few helpful hinds and then the link to your create space page. We'll also use You Tube for the same thing. We can then 'monotize' both your blog and You tube to create 'spin-off' income in the form af advertisiments using Google's AdSense program.

Lety's summerise the process so far:
- We've created a book or DVD and self-published it using Create Space. (that's one income stream)
- We've then uploaded it to Kindle (that's two income streams)
- We'll then create links to your eStore from Blogger and You Tube with advertsiments to further supplement your income.

That's three income streams and two extrnal links and we've only just started. You haven't even had to outlay a dollar and you've created an income!

Stage Two

In the previous chapter we created a book or DVD using Create Space and published it on both Amazon and Kindle. An important process is to create external links to further promote your material.
For this stage we'll open an account with AdSense, You Tube and Blogger.
By the time you have worked through this book you'll have created over twenty income streams and that means a lot a new accounts with passwords.
Contrary to the advice from IT experts, you can't have the same passwords for everything so we suggest you use a spreadsheet to store log-in details and passwords.

Also, some of the accounts we open go through an approval process to check where you will be placing advertsiments so we'll start with Blogger and create links back to your Create Space eStore before we apply for advertisments or Affiliate programs.

Open a new browser screen and simply go to the Google Home page. Google Blogger works best with Google "Chrome"

From Google's home p
click on the 'More' tab
click on "Blogger"

From here we can open a new account

This will open a new screen to sign up for a Blogger Account. Click on the red "Sign Up" button on the top right hand side of the screen and follow through the process. You'll also need to create a Gmail account.

Once you've completed this step, start again from the Google home page and create a You Tube account as well.

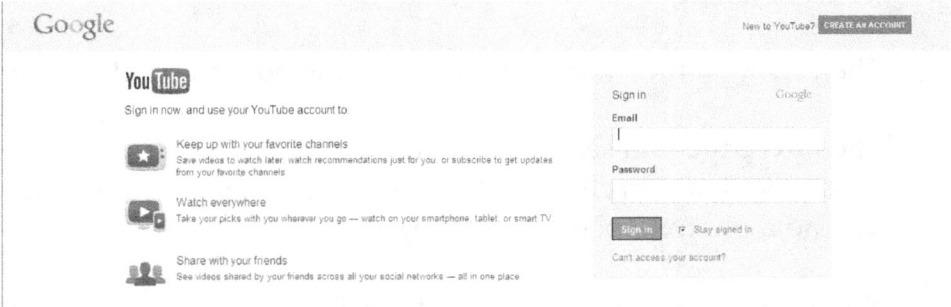

If the name you choose is not available, just keep trying different names until you find one that is available.

Once you find a Google 'username' you'll need to create a password to protect your account. You need to use at least 8 characters. Remember not to use a password from another site, or something too obvious like your pet's name

You've almost finished the first step...
Moving down the page, fill in your birthday, gender, phone number and the email address that you normally use (not the one you created above)

Once you're done, move down the page to confirm your country of location with the 'drop down box' and then you'll need to click on the box that says

"I agree to the Google **Terms of Service** *and* **Privacy Policy"**

(You won't be able to move forward if you don't agree to the terms of use)

Then click on the 'next step' button at the bottome of the page.

The next page you see will be your profile.
If you like you can click on the 'add profile photo' button and upload a photo to personalise your profile

You'll then get on-screen instructions if you would like to crop or create effects for your profile picture.

Remember that this profile is public so everybody will be able to see your name and photo. (You can change this later if you're not happy with your profile being public.)
When you're happy with your profile picture, click on the 'next step' button.

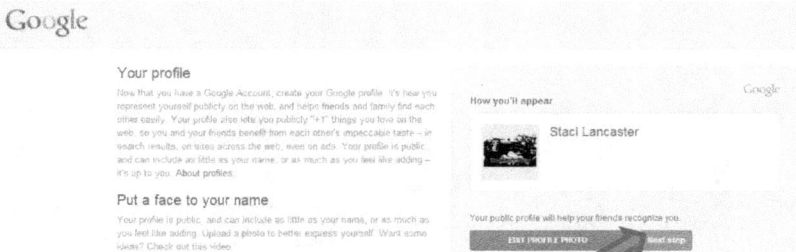

You'll then come to the 'welcome' screen.

That's the end of step one and the beginning of a whole lot of fun!

Go back to the Google home page and click on the 'You Tube' button.

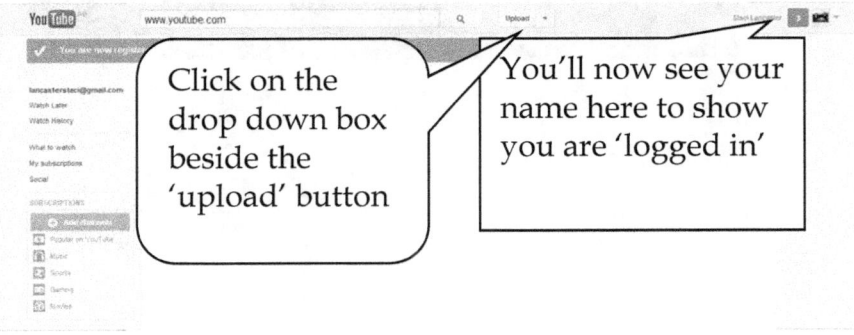

You're now able to register with **You Tube** and log in!

Next Click on the drop down box beside the 'upload' button

Note: On the previous page we mentioned changing your profile if you're not happy using your real name.

There is a little trick to this.

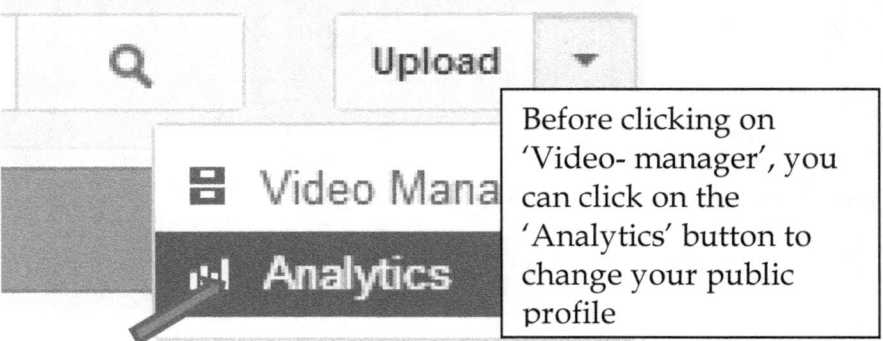

Before clicking on 'Video- manager', you can click on the 'Analytics' button to change your public profile

Let's keep going, click on the 'OK, I'm ready to contingue' button and you'll be taken to your personal home page (also called your landing screen)

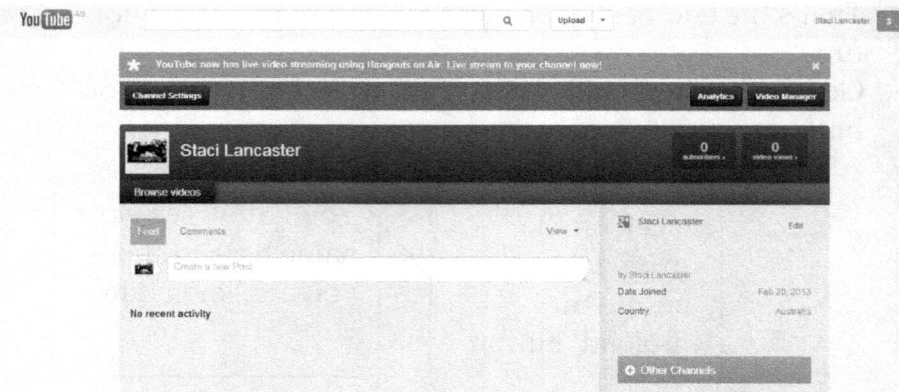

Surprise Secret idea

Let's jump ahead to some really exciting ideas...
Did you know that you don't even need a camera to make
You tube videos?

We didn't meantion it earlier because firstly we wanted to
surprise you and second, people probably wouldn't believe it.

You can very easily make animated movies that move and
speak. You can use your own voice or use an animated voice.

To have a look, click on the 'Brouse Videos' button (even
though we don't have any yet)

We'll cover this in more detail later but while on on this page,
have a quick look. Scroll down the blue drop down boxes...

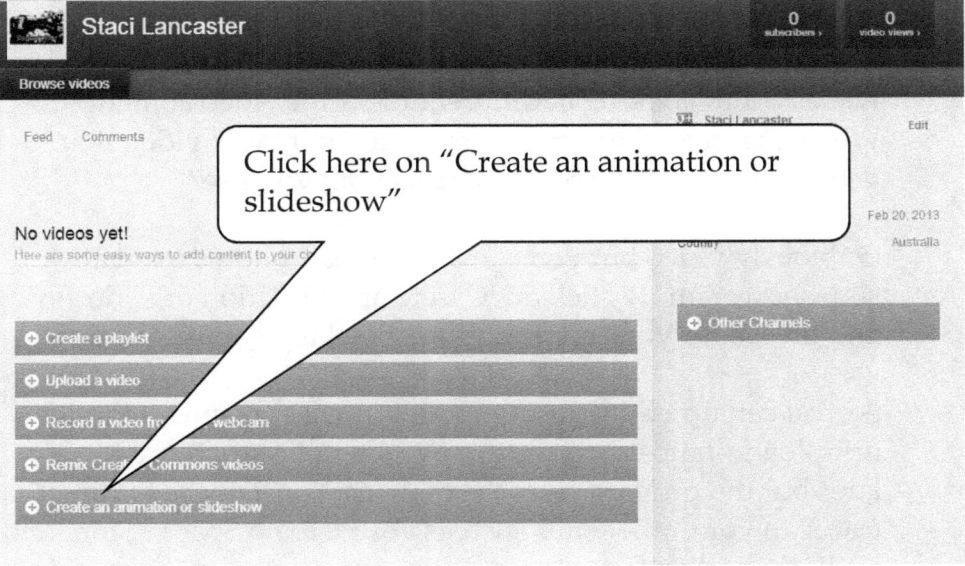

There are several different modes (or providers) that you can use. We find "Go Animate" is great but it's not free! You can play around and make animated videos but if you want to use it for making money then you'll have to subcribe to Go Animate Commercial version that currently costs US$50 a month. If you don't have other 'real' video content but you have great ideas then it can be a good way to get started.

Keep it fun while you learn and play around with animation. It might give you some great ideas

The next step is making and uploading your video. Let's start by looking at different ideas for video content. We've just seen that you can make an animated video that gets your message across, what else can you use?

Ovbiously video but you can also upload photos to create a slideshow. Simply click on 'Create an animation or slideshow' and browe for your photos. (They need to be in jPeg format)

So you can upload your own video, create an animated video or upload photos for a slideshow. We'll discuss more ideas later but the primary purpose of using You Tube is to direct traffic to your other sites such as your Create Space eStore and affiliate products.

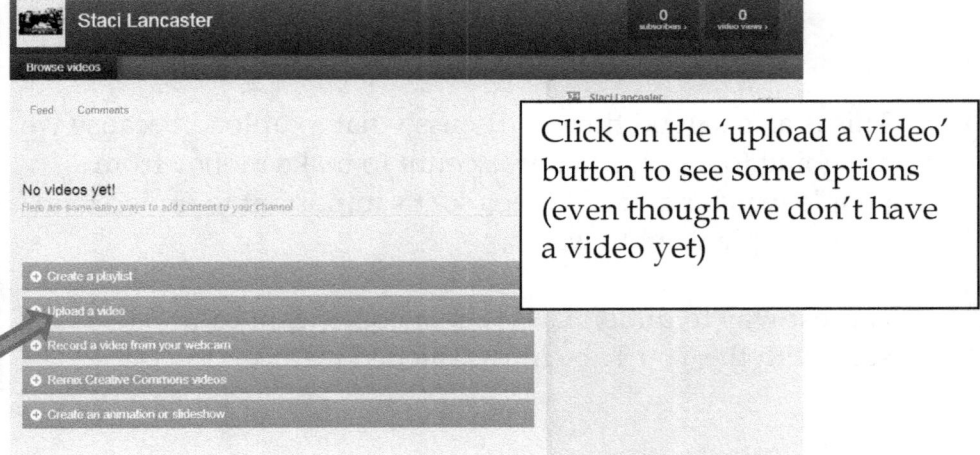

Click on the 'upload a video' button to see some options (even though we don't have a video yet)

This will give you some options and more ideas...

1. Upload video that you have filmed yourself
2. Upload animated video that you created using Go Animate or one of the several other providers
3. Create a photo slide show (see the next step)
4. A combination of the above three

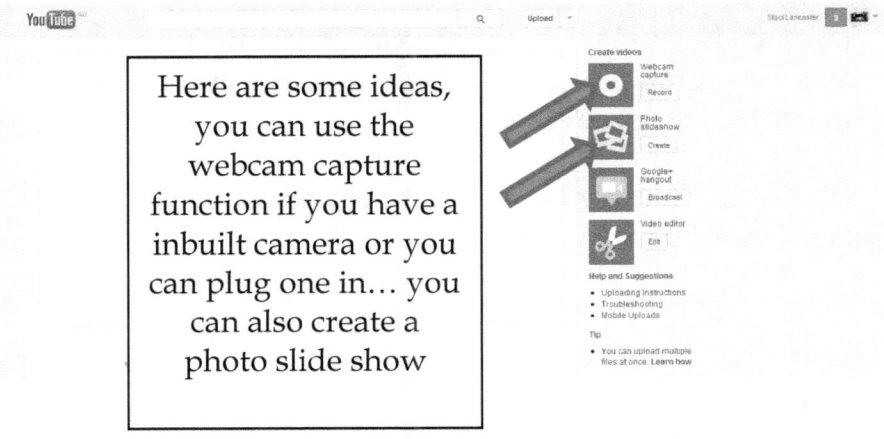

Here are some ideas, you can use the webcam capture function if you have a inbuilt camera or you can plug one in... you can also create a photo slide show

It's time to upload some video content then we'll also look at creating a video slideshow

This is also a good time to discuss what to upload because we are going to monitize your account to make money from people watching your videos so it's important to understand what people want to watch.

A great way to understand what people want to watch is to start with the You Tube most watched feature

Best of YouTube

From your home page, click on 'popular on you tube' to see what is getting the most views.

In one word, it has to be entertaining...

You can now use You Tube to create an income from advertising or to direct traffic to your other paying sites such as your Create Space eStore.

Let's go back to your blogger account and create links back to your Create Space eStore.

Extra Money's blogs

We have enabled automatic spam detection for comments. You should occasionally check the comments in your spam inbox. Learn m
Blogger's spam detection or report issues.

New Blog

Country and Outdoors
36 pageviews · 7 posts · last published on 20-Mar-2013

50 Ways that people make Extra Money for Addit...
224 pageviews · 26 posts · last published on 14-Mar-2013

View blog

> From your blogger page you can create a new post

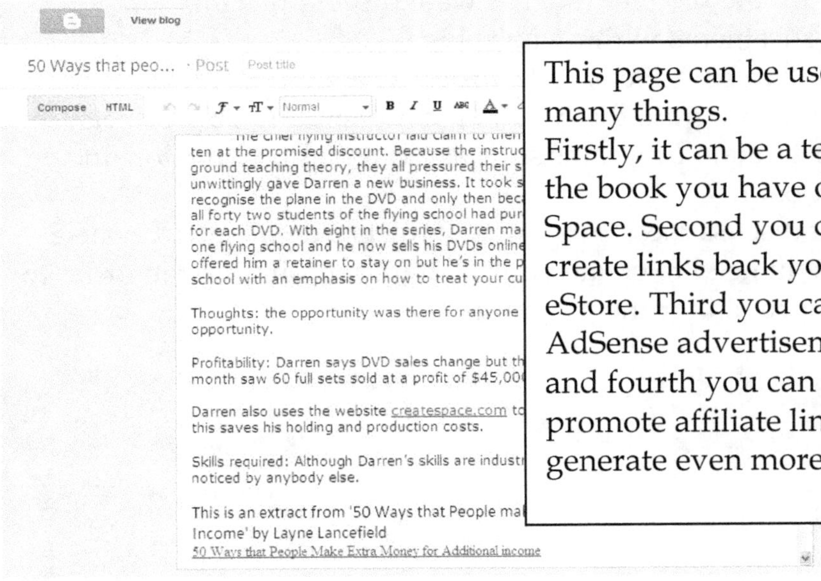

Reading list | All blogs

Add

All blogs

Blogger Buzz

Add blogs to follow in your Reading List
You are not currently following any blogs. Use the "Add" button to enter blogs that you'd like to follow in your Reading List.
Learn more

View blog

50 Ways that peo... · Post   Post title

Compose   HTML   𝓕 ▾ 𝔗 ▾ Normal   ▾ B I U ABC A ▾

The chief flying instructor laid claim to their
ten at the promised discount. Because the instruc
ground teaching theory, they all pressured their s
unwittingly gave Darren a new business. It took s
recognise the plane in the DVD and only then bec
all forty two students of the flying school had pur
for each DVD. With eight in the series, Darren ma
one flying school and he now sells his DVDs online
offered him a retainer to stay on but he's in the p
school with an emphasis on how to treat your cu

Thoughts: the opportunity was there for anyone
opportunity.

Profitability: Darren says DVD sales change but th
month saw 60 full sets sold at a profit of $45,000

Darren also uses the website createspace.com to
this saves his holding and production costs.

Skills required: Although Darren's skills are industr
noticed by anybody else.

This is an extract from '50 Ways that People ma
Income' by Layne Lancefield
50 Ways that People Make Extra Money for Additional income

> This page can be used for many things.
> Firstly, it can be a teaser for the book you have on Create Space. Second you can create links back your own eStore. Third you can run AdSense advertisements and fourth you can use it to promote affiliate links to generate even more income.

To create a link on your Blog post, click on the "link" tab on the blogger tool bar.

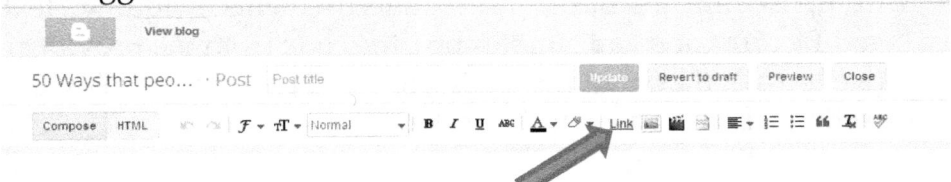

View blog

50 Ways that peo... · Post   Post title   Update Revert to draft Preview Close

Compose   HTML   𝓕 ▾ 𝔗 ▾ Normal   ▾ B I U ABC A ▾ Link

This will open a new box as below.

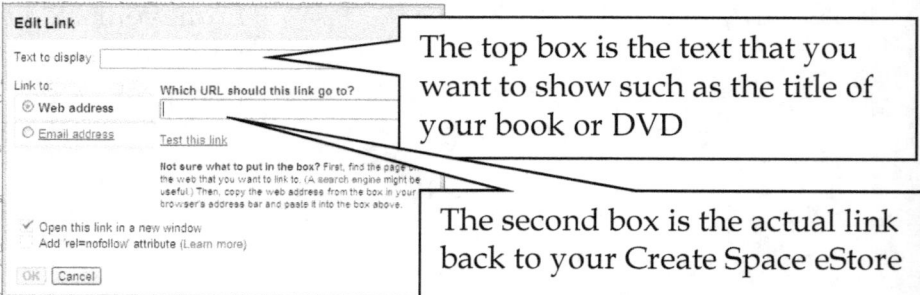

The top box is the text that you want to show such as the title of your book or DVD

The second box is the actual link back to your Create Space eStore

Back on the Blogger tool bar we'll discuss placing advertisements within your blog.

These can be AdSense ads, products from the Amazon Affiliate program that you're recommending or products from other affiliate programs such as Commission Junction and Click Bank.

We'll discuss these programs in further detail later because you will need to create your blog (or website) first in order to be approved for the programs.

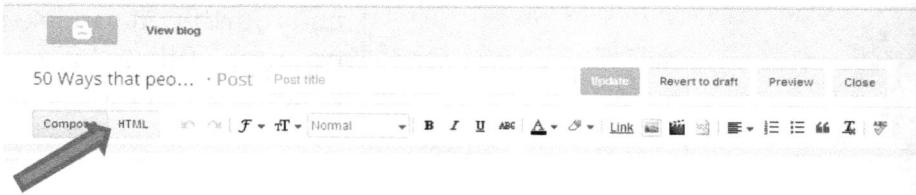

You'll notice the "compose" and "HTML" tabs. Unless you're a programmer, you'll be typing all your blog posts in the Compose function but to insert advertisements including "text and Picture" ads you simple copy the code from the provider (we'll cover that in more detail later) and paste in the HTML section where you want the add to appear.

Let's take a moment to summarize:

- We've created a book or DVD and uploaded it Create Space to Sell on Amazon
- We also uploaded your book to Kindle
- We've created a Blog to direct traffic to our Create Space eStore with advertisements as 'spin off' income
- We've also created You Tube videos, slideshows or tutorials to direct traffic to our eStore as well as AdSense ads for 'spin off' income.
- Our blog will also contain affiliate links from companies such as Commission Junction, Click bank, Link Share and the Amazon Affiliate program just to name a few.

We have still only scratched the surface but already you can identify half a dozen income streams just from creating links or legs to supply other income streams.

Stage Three

Affiliate Programs.

Affiliate programs are more than just advertisements; they let you sell a specific product without having to buy or handle it. The reason we created a blog first was because most programs will check the blog or website to be sure it's not unsuitable material such as 'hate' or pornographic content.

These affiliate links can be used in many creative ways. The Amazon Affiliate program allows you to sell anything that's on the Amazon website from books to boots and televisions to scuba gear.

You will be given a unique code that you can simply imbed in almost any digital media.

We discussed the HTML tab in Blogger to insert text and media ads. From the Affiliate programs you simple copy the code and paste it where you want the ad to appear. You can then write a review on the product to recommend it and you'll be paid a commission every time somebody clicks on your link to buy it.

Let's jump ahead and look at a website we've built that is purely affiliate marketing and content ads.

Our website is **www.scubaapparatus.com** and at the time of writing it is listed as number seven on the first page of Google when you search for both words 'Scuba' and 'Apparatus' .

Scroll further down the page…

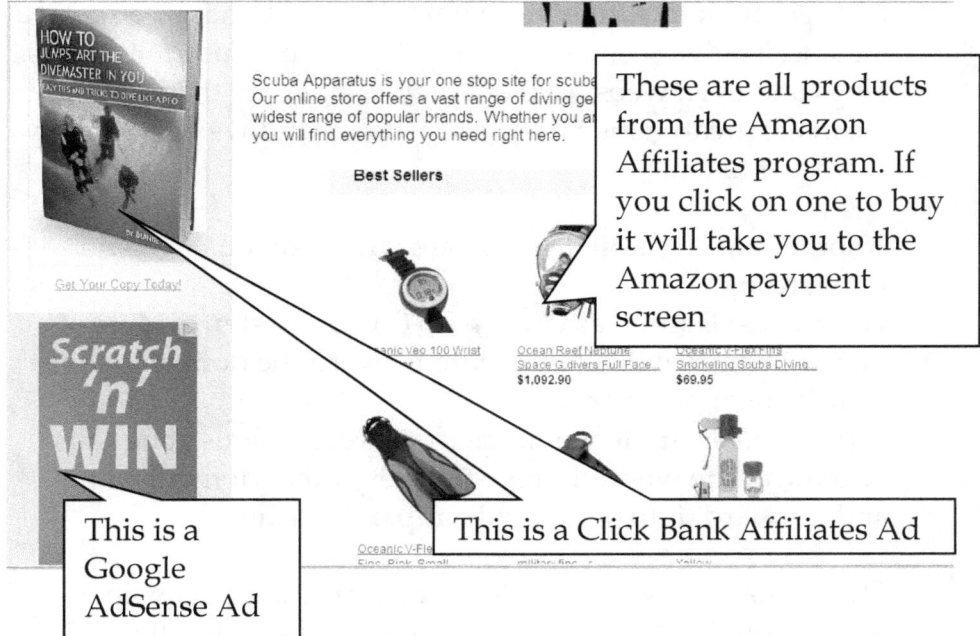

You can see we don't have any maintenance with this website. The last page you looked at on our **www.scubaapparatus.com** website had three income streams just on that page. If you scroll down you'll see it says "Powered by Amazon" that's how you know it's an affiliate ad but it also gives people peace of mind knowing they have the security of buying through the Amazon Secure Website.

The website was built using Webnode - **http://www.webnode.com/business-websites/** If you scroll to the bottom of the **www.scubaapparatus.com** website you'll see a link (no it's not an affiliate link, it can be removed but we left it there as a reference for you)

Webnode is an easy 'drag and click' website building program that we'll cover in more detail later.

Let's get back to Affiliate Programs as they'll make you a great income. You've seen how affiliate links can be used in emails, blogs and even websites that are nothing more than ads but we make great money from that website and we've got many more just like it.

Another idea for affiliate links are what's called "Domain Forwarding"
We use 'Go Daddy' as it's easy to do but most providers of domain names will allow you to forward the domain onto a website of another name.
A practical example would be if we were serious about our Scuba website we could register every other domain name and 'forward' it to **www.scubaapparatus.com.**

The Domain Forwarding idea in advertising affiliate links means you don't even need to build a website. We'll use Go Daddy as an example, **(www.godaddy.com)** because they have a great local assistance program as do Smarty Host **(www.smartyhost.com.au**). Once you've registered a domain name you can go to the 'Advanced' function under Domain Forwarding and create key search words in relation to the product you're recommending.
Sure this will cost you a couple of dollars, about $3 a year! Here's a tip, before you buy from Go Daddy check out the Fat Wallet website for discount codes **www.fatwallet.com**

Next we'll create a website to sign up for some affiliate programs.

We'll use Webnode - **http://www.webnode.com/business-websites/** as it's easy to use and also supplies some content.

Sign up to get started

There are two ways you can start, either by creating a domain name or creating a website first.

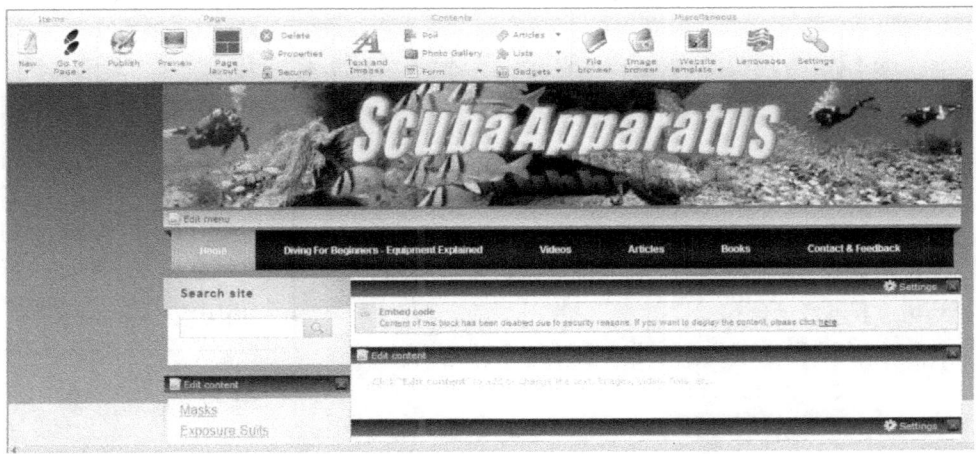

Here we are inside the 'Control Panel' of our website Scuba Apparatus. The tool bar at the top has drag and click functions to add new features such as advertising panels.

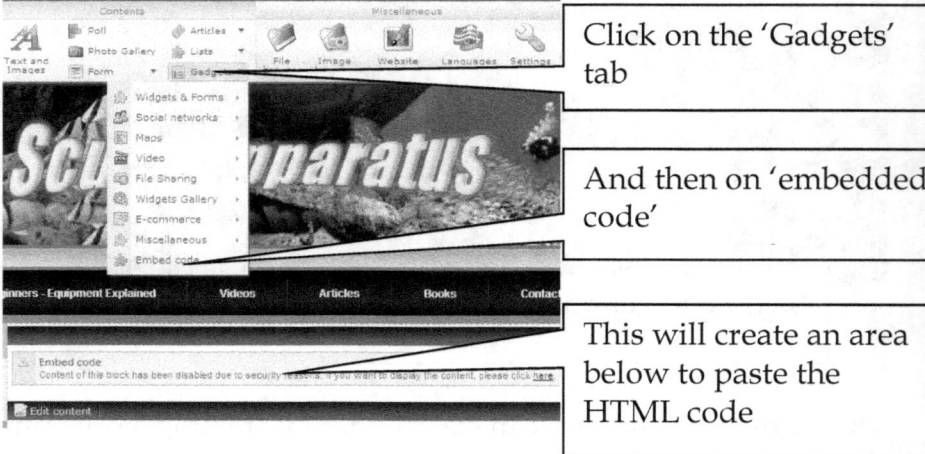

Click on the 'Gadgets' tab

And then on 'embedded code'

This will create an area below to paste the HTML code

You can then drag this box to other areas of the website.

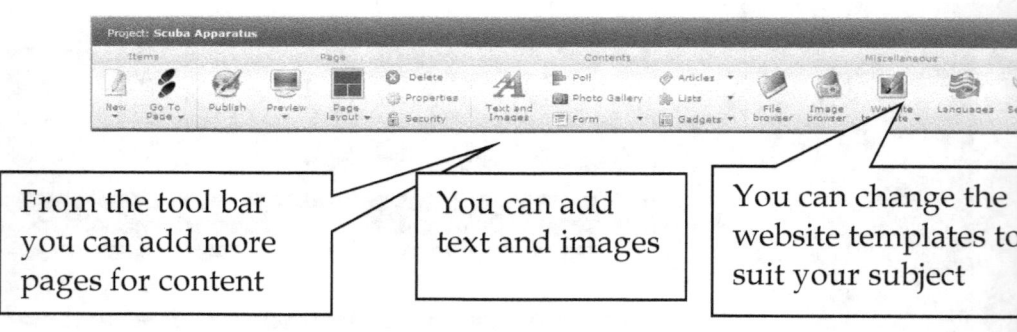

From the tool bar you can add more pages for content

You can add text and images

You can change the website templates to suit your subject

Once you have a website or a blog constructed you can start applying to affiliate and advertising programs.

Let's start with the three we used for the Scuba website:

- Amazon
- Google AdSense and
- Clickbank.

From the Google
home page search for
Google AdSense

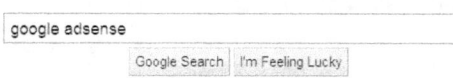

google adsense

Google Search   I'm Feeling Lucky

It's a similar process to sign up and register as we did for both
the Gmail account and You Tube.

When your AdSense account is approved, log in and click on
'My Ads'

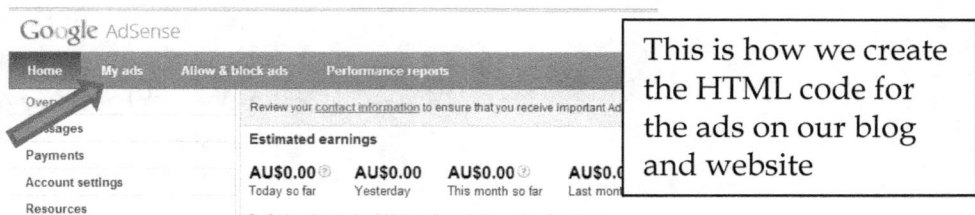

This is how we create
the HTML code for
the ads on our blog
and website

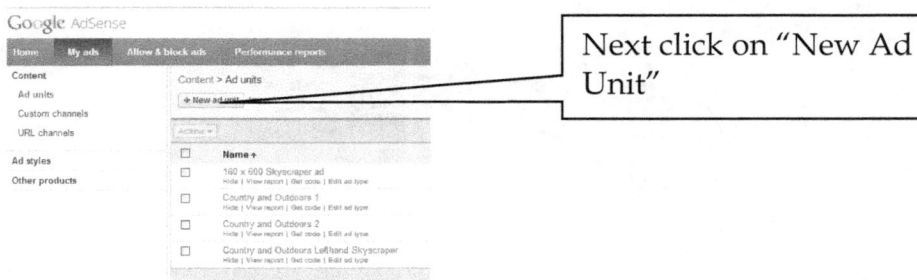

Next click on "New Ad
Unit"

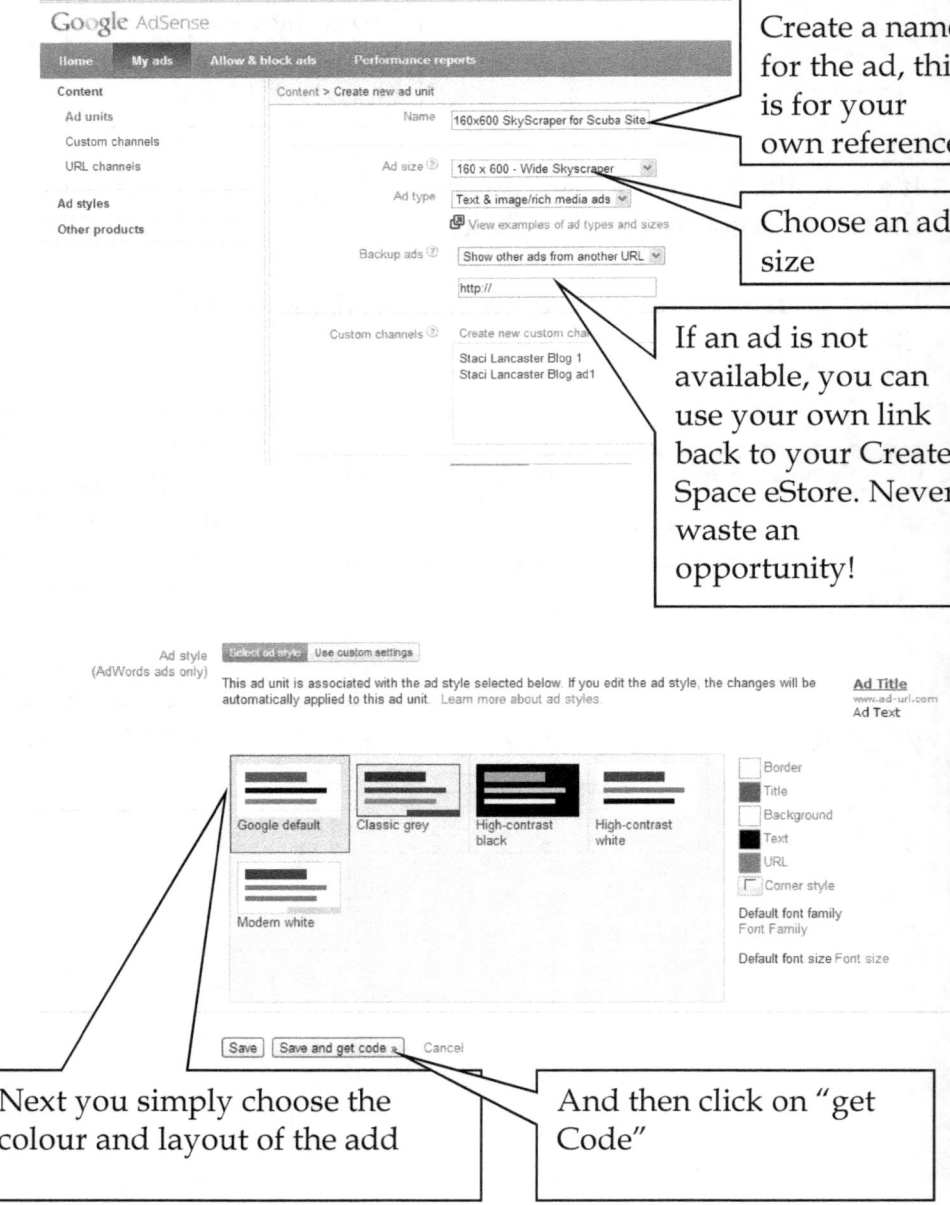

Create a name for the ad, this is for your own reference

Choose an ad size

If an ad is not available, you can use your own link back to your Create Space eStore. Never waste an opportunity!

Next you simply choose the colour and layout of the add

And then click on "get Code"

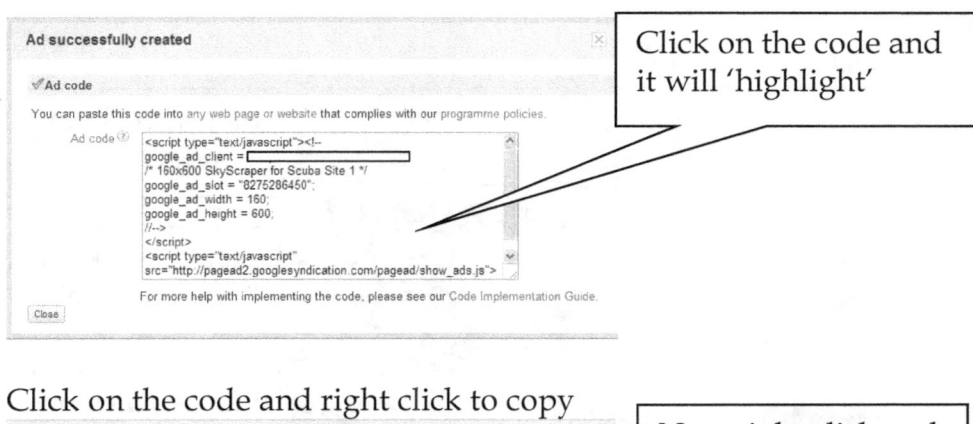

Click on the code and it will 'highlight'

Click on the code and right click to copy

Next right click and copy the code

Now let's go back to our Webnode website construction page (page 34)

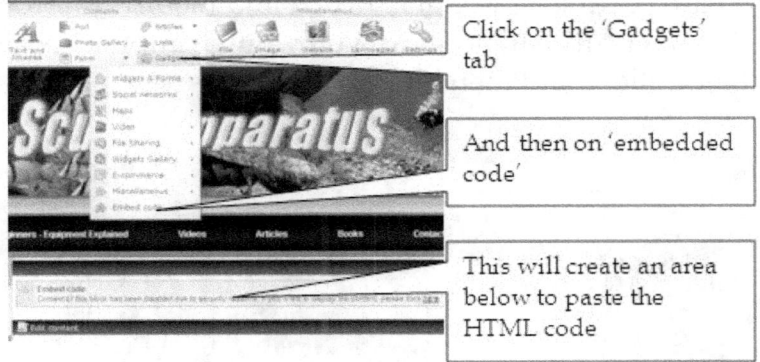

Click on the 'Gadgets' tab

And then on 'embedded code'

This will create an area below to paste the HTML code

You might have to repeat the steps we covered above.

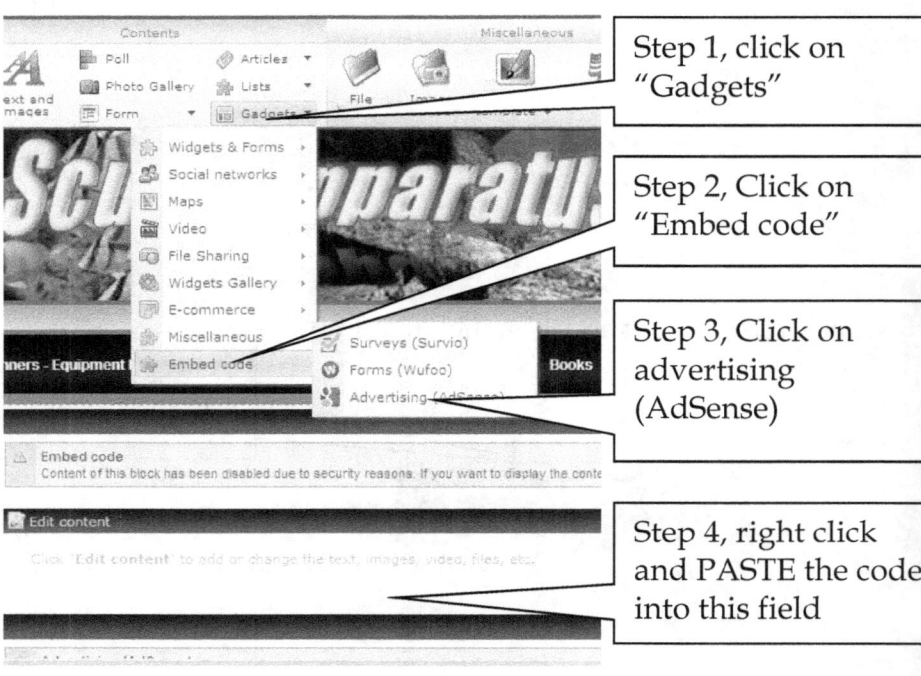

You can then move this box to where you want the ad to appear.

If you are pasting a "Widget" (a text and picture ad) from say the Amazon Affiliate program you would simply choose Widget Gallery and then 'Other Widget'

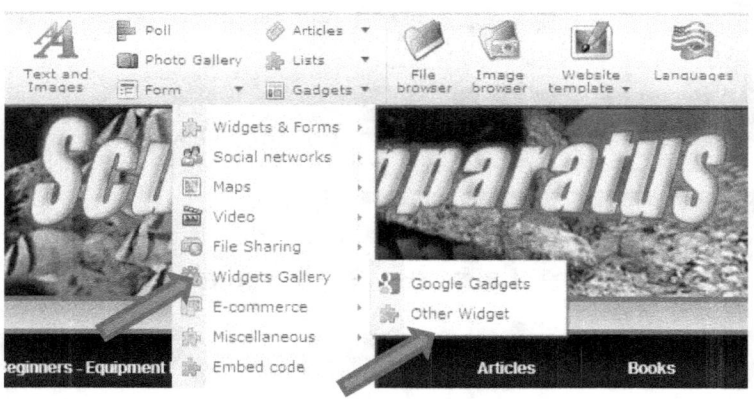

Now simply right click and paste the code into the area you created.

You can then drag this box to other areas of your website where you want the "Widget" to be placed.

Congratulations, you are now a certified programmer, computer geek and online income receiving entrepreneur!

You now know how to program a website, create and apply HTML code and you also have a few new income streams.

Let's now apply to the Amazon, Clickbank and Commission Junction Affiliate Programs.
There is a brief approval period for each one which is why we created a blog and website first.

Go to Amazon.com and scroll down to the bottom of the page where you'll see a link for "Become an affiliate"

Get to Know Us
Careers
Investor Relations
Press Releases
Amazon and Our Planet
Amazon in the Community

Make Money with Us
Sell on Amazon
Become an Affiliate
Advertise Your Products
Independently Publish with Us
› See all

Let Us Help You
Your Account
Shipping Rates & Policies
Amazon Prime
Returns Are Easy
Manage Your Kindle
Customer Service

amazon.com

Brazil   Canada   China   France   Germany   Italy   Japan   Spain   United Kingdom

By now you can work your way through a registration page, it's pretty simple so we'll skip through to the approval email.

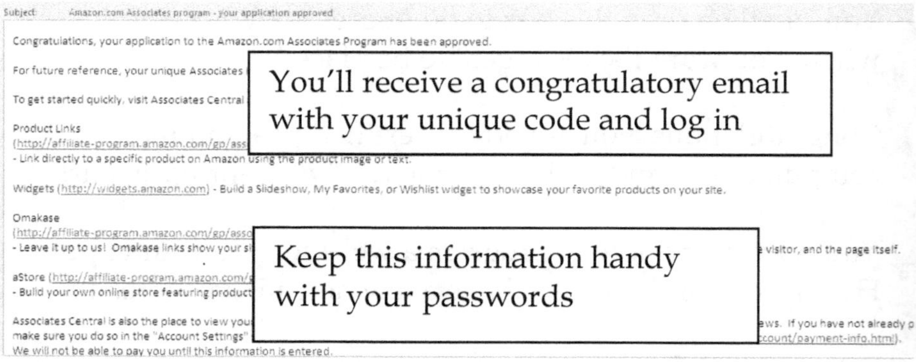

Subject: Amazon.com Associates program - your application approved

Congratulations, your application to the Amazon.com Associates Program has been approved.

For future reference, your unique Associates

To get started quickly, visit Associates Central

Product Links
(http://affiliate-program.amazon.com/gp/ass
- Link directly to a specific product on Amazon using the product image or text.

Widgets (http://widgets.amazon.com) - Build a Slideshow, My Favorites, or Wishlist widget to showcase your favorite products on your site.

Omakase
(http://affiliate-program.amazon.com/gp/ass
- Leave it up to us! Omakase links show your si

aStore (http://affiliate-program.amazon.com/
- Build your own online store featuring product

Associates Central is also the place to view you
make sure you do so in the "Account Settings"
We will not be able to pay you until this information is entered.

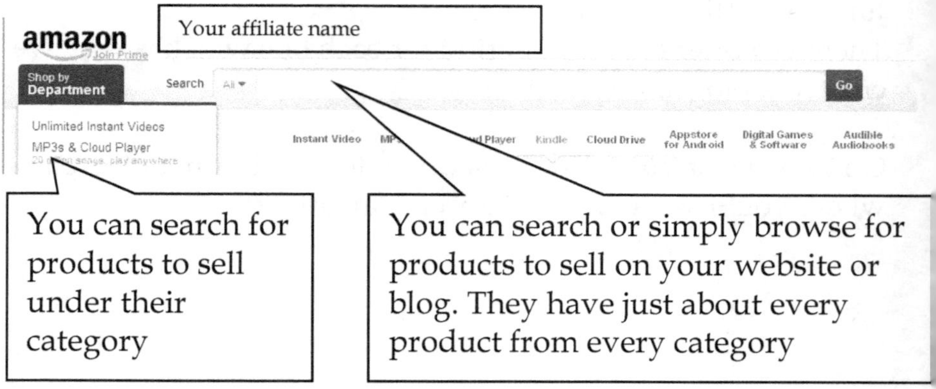

> You'll receive a congratulatory email with your unique code and log in

> Keep this information handy with your passwords

amazon

> Your affiliate name

Shop by Department   Search   All ▾   Go

Unlimited Instant Videos
MP3s & Cloud Player

Instant Video   MP3   ...Player   Kindle   Cloud Drive   Appstore for Android   Digital Games & Software   Audible Audiobooks

> You can search for products to sell under their category

> You can search or simply browse for products to sell on your website or blog. They have just about every product from every category

When you find a product that you want to sell, you will generate a code in a similar way to the Google AdSense code.

Let's say we want to promote and sell a Scuba knife on our Scuba website.

Find the product you want to promote and click on it.

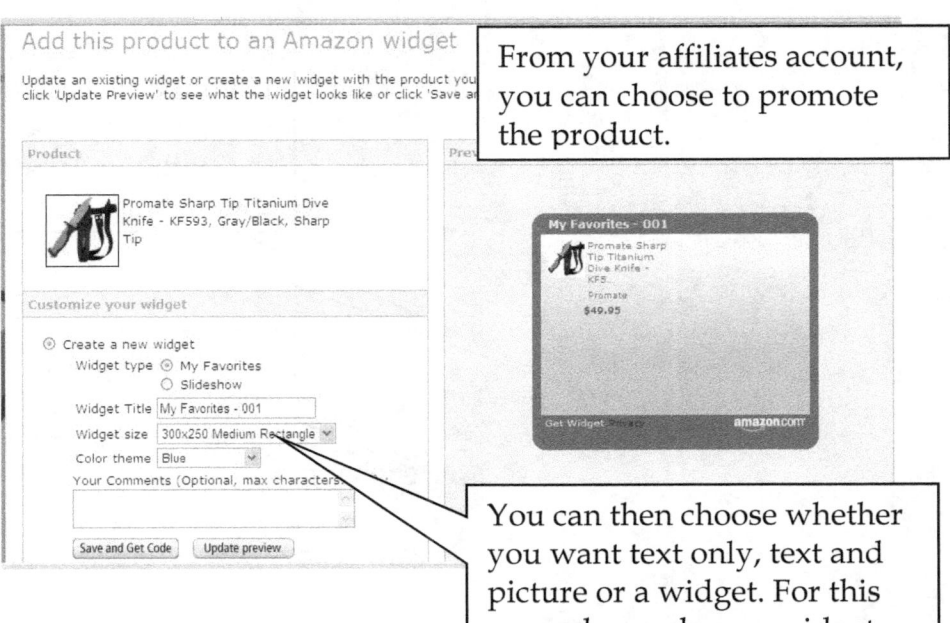

From your affiliates account, you can choose to promote the product.

You can then choose whether you want text only, text and picture or a widget. For this example we chose a widget

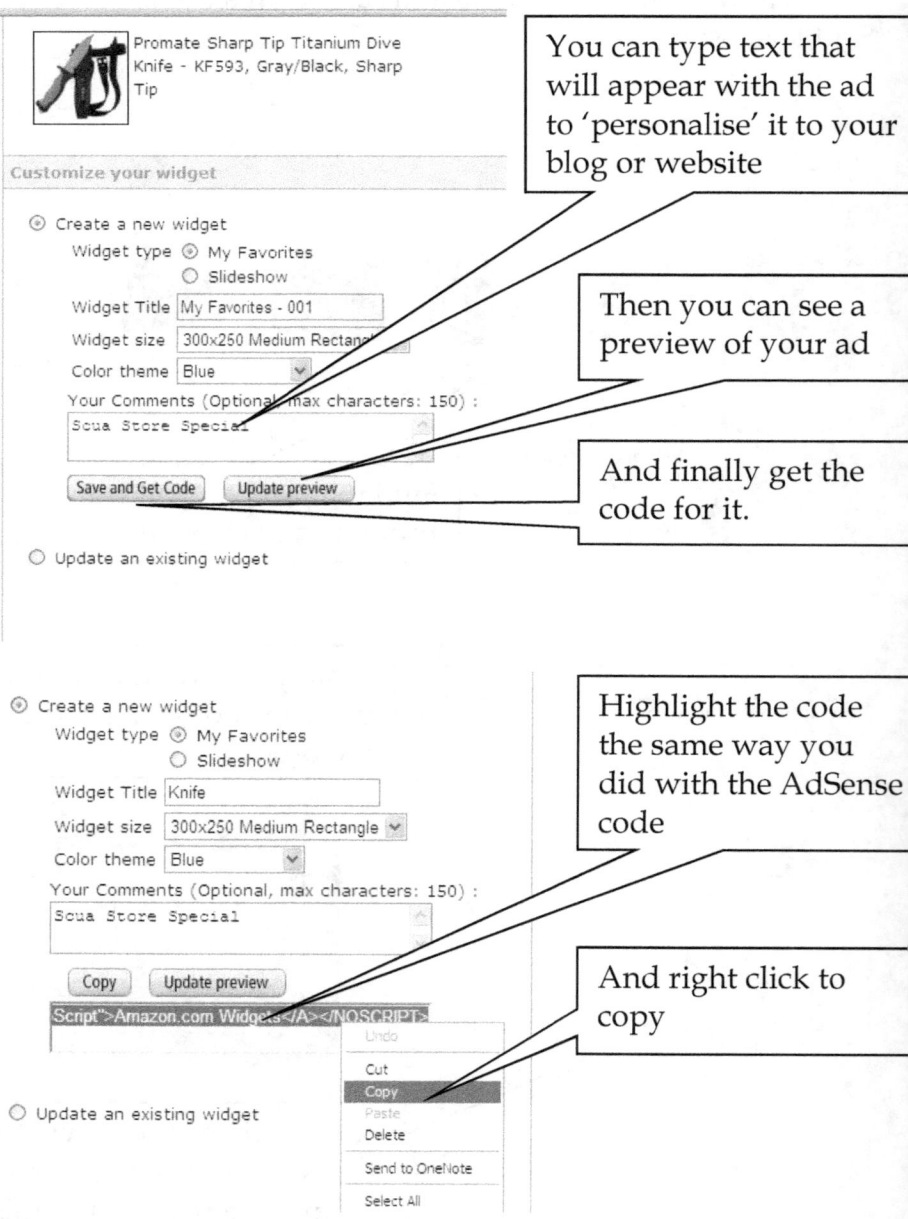

You now have the HTML code to paste into your website or blog where you want the ad to appear.

Let's go ahead and sign up with both Clickbank and Commission Junction.

We'll use different Affiliate programs for several reasons;

1. They all have different products
2. They have different commission structures and
3. It will give your site or blog some variation.

Commission Junction is great for referring people to websites such as Create Space to be a self-publisher. If you are writing a blog you can put a Commission Junction link (CJ Link) into your blog and recommend it. You will receive a referral fee of $8 for anybody who clicks through and opens an account. Not bad considering it's free to join Create Space! In the same way you could refer people to the GoDaddy website with a code so that you earn up to $493 for a referral through Commission Junction (**www.jc.com**) or Linkshare (**linkshare.com**)

ClickBank, on the other hand is for digital products such as programs and exclusive website access. These affiliate links pay up to 75% commission for a click through and sale.

Let's summarize what we've learned to this point;

- We understand how to self-publish through Amazon's sister site Create Space and Kindle as well as ideas using Public Domain work, gathering our own through creativity and interviewing people as well as out-sourcing through companies such as Get Friday.
- We can build a simple website or blog that can create income by referring back to our Create Space eStore as well as creating its own income through ads and affiliate links.
- We can use email, social media such as Facebook and twitter to promote our material.

- We understand the concept of "Domain Forwarding" to advertise products with our unique code without even using a website or blog.
- We understand how to copy and paste HTML code like as if we're computer geniuses and…
- We can create an ongoing income that's passive, sustainable and has not cost a cent!

The important points to remember are that although it's great creating an income using all these techniques, it's when you link them together that they become powerful. This is when they begin to compound or snowball and your income grows exponentially!

To this point we have created a product through Create Space and Kindle that's producing two income streams for us. AdSense has monetized our blog and You Tube referral programs creating another couple of income streams.
The Amazon, Clickbank, Commission Junction and Linkshare affiliate programs bring that income stream up to ten separate income streams that have the dual purpose of referring leads as well as producing their own income.

Before we move on, using some creativity you can multiply your income by creating more books, DVDs, CD,s or MP3s to publish (in other words, using more building blocks) or you can keep expanding on the referrals of current products (in other words make the building blocks bigger)

An example of 'more building blocks' would be us creating more and more websites such as our
www.scubaapparatus.com website that simply creates an ongoing income from affiliate ads. The cost of this website is about twelve dollars a year for the domain name registration.

That concludes our 'overview' of creating an online income. The next chapter expands on what you've learned without going over the basics of creating accounts and signing up for new programs.

If you're a beginner, hopefully by now you can see how easy it is to create a website or a blog and generate HTML code that produces ads and affiliate referrals making online income for you.

Next we will expand on other 'Primary' income generators and further link what we have produced. Linking our websites and blogs not only increases traffic and thereby increases our profit margins but it also increases the Google search engine results as one of the analyzers for Google depends on how many 'incoming' links you have to your website.

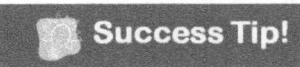

The reason these exersises have been spread out over ten days is because as a bigginer it's a lot of new work. Keep yourself positive by taking breaks and only speak about your projects with like minded people who will encourage you to keep pushing forward!

Be creative and explore other providers, we used Webnode because of it's simplicity but you should also check out GoDaddy and SmartyHost to name a couple.

Google the term "Affiliate Programs" and you'll see there are many more programs to help expand your online income.

Stage Four

Let's cover some more 'Primary income' generators such as the Create Space book we published.

You can also publish your book on LuLu (**www.lulu.com**)

This will help further distibute the material you've already created.

When your book really takes off, you'll find Lighting Source **http://www1.lightningsource.com/** a great resource for POD (Print on demand) of smaller print runs.

With Lulu and Lighting source you have the ability to create more professional covers with different bindings and cover sleves.

If you have photography skills you'll do well to create material for iStock Photo.**www.istockphoto.com**

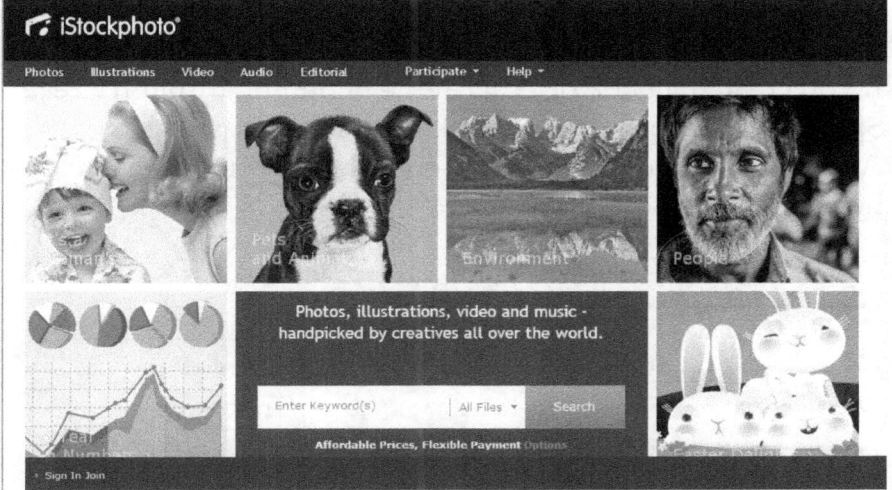

You don't need expensive equipment but iStock photo won't accept rubbish either. The website has a tutorial that discribes the quality that they're looking for, we didn't get accepted the first few times so it takes some work but the commissions make it worth the effort.

Café Press is another one for creativity, like Amazon it caters for your primary products that you can create and upload as well as the affiliate program (**www.cafepress.com.au**)

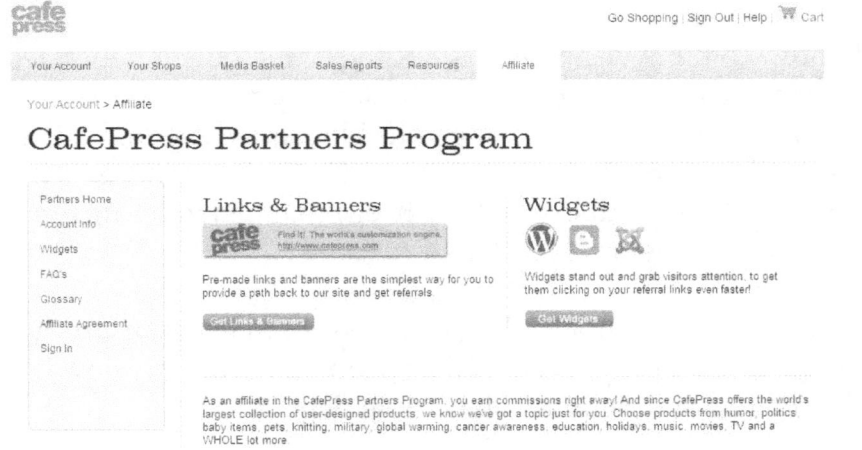

If you created a book or DVD at the biginning through Create Space, you can be both a suppllier for Programs such as Amazon Affiliates as well as user of the products. This further helps promote your products.

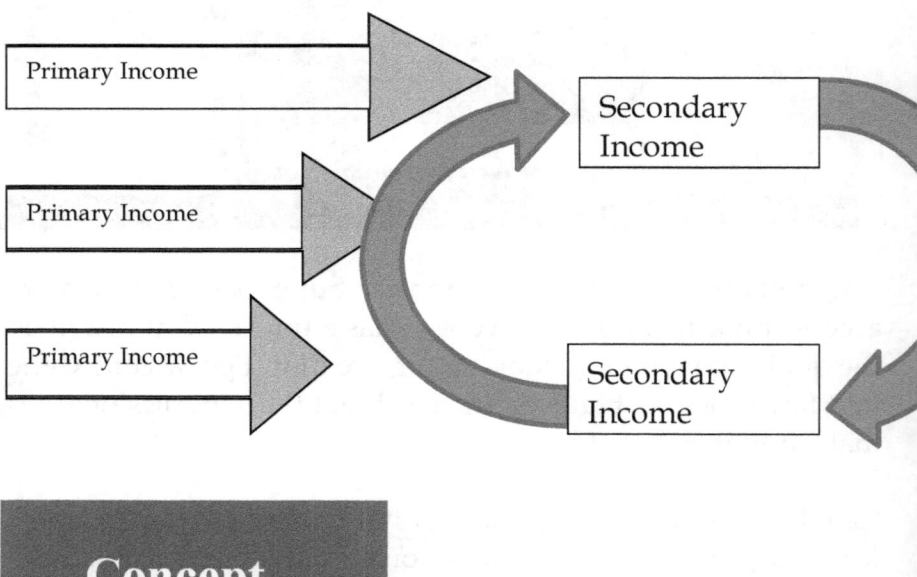

Concept

By now you'll have an understanding of the power generated by creating links that both refer back to a primary product such as Create Space by using your blog as a teaser of your Create Space product and the spin off income generated by the secondary product (the blog itself) that generates income through AdSense and Affiliate Programs.

To deepen this compounding effect, you can list your product on the affiliate program for other people to promote, now your compounding model has triple depth.

You primary products, the products you have produced yourself usually produce the highest income.

One factor to increase the compounding of your income is to increrase the primary contributors.

Café Press (**www.cafepress.com**) allows you to upload a design onto just about anything from T Shirts to Coffee mugs.

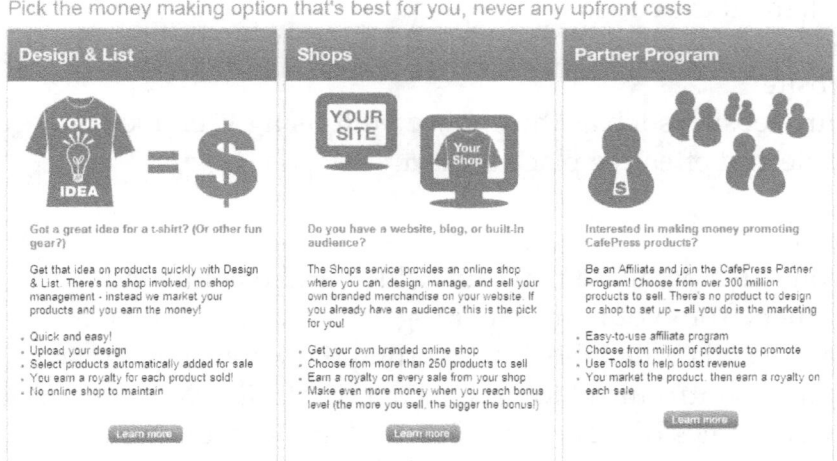

Upload your design to the website and you can earn a royalty for each product sold. Again, just like your Create Space products, your creativity and dedication to some work is what'll pay you an income.

You can also create links back to your blog or website to sell the designs you create.

Third, you can become an Affiliate and join the CafePress Partner Program. Choose from over 300 million products to sell. If creativity and design are not your forte, you can just do the marketing.

Café Press adds three more strings to the bow of your on-line income toolbox.

Let's dig deeper into the use of Affiliate links. We've covered the set up, implementation and expansion of both Amazon and AdSense code so you'll be able to work out how to use the code from Commission Junction (**www.cj.com**) and Click bank (**www.clickbank.com**) but there are many ways you can implement the code.

Website
Your website, such as the one we built using Webnode is a simple and effective place to start.

Email
If you run a database you can include and recommend products from your Affiliate Program. Staci and Layne interviewed Craig who, by attending the wrong conference room was introduced to the concept of Affiliate Marketing. As National Sales Manager of a financial and accounting products company, he has over 5000 sales people on his email database.
The database is not actualy his but his job includes writing and sending out an email newletter every Monday morning and so every week he recommends a new product from Amazon. Whether it's the latest and greatest calculator that makes compounding interest easy to calculate or the latest book exlaining how to use the software he recommended the previous week, his affiliate income is the most exciting part of his job. Craig says Monday mornings have become his favorite day of the week.

Let's look at some of the different ways to use affiliate programs. We've discusssed the Amazon program in some details so let's concentrate on Click bank (**www.clickbank.com**)

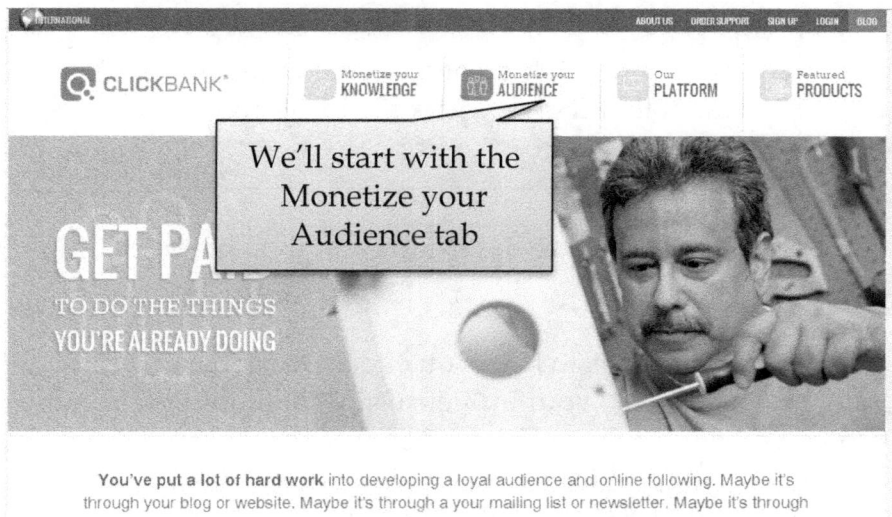

You can also use Click Bank to sell your own products such as a eBook but we'll start by getting paid to recommend other people's products.

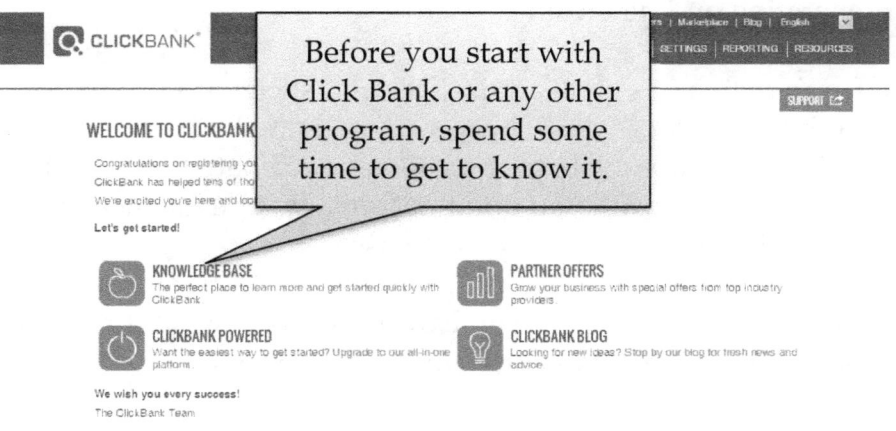

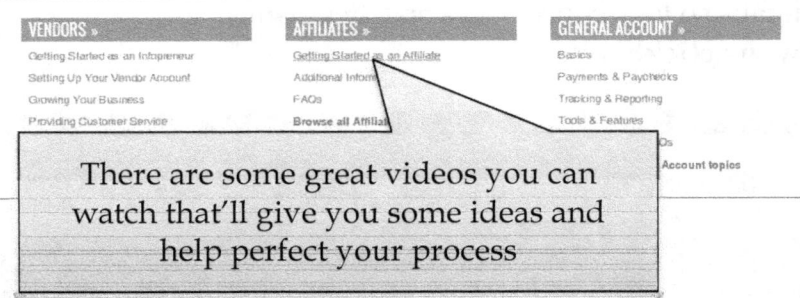

There are some great videos you can watch that'll give you some ideas and help perfect your process

Click on the "Knowledge Base" tabe and then go to 'Getting Started as an Affiliate'.

There are four videos to help you choose your niche, built your platform, grow your audience and then how to promote products.
They have a helpful list of recommended resourses to help you build a succsessful on-line buisness that's a lot more than just a hobby.

Put these videos to use as training programs to accelerate your learning, block out time in your diary to become an expert at generating on-line income.

"Don't rush in" is great advice. Try and stick with products that interest you as this'll keep you motivated. There are many Affiliate Prgrams avaliable (just Google Affiliate Programs) but to be succseesful you don't need many, you just need to master the few that you choose to use.

You'll then need to make some decisions as to what direction you want to take regarding your business model.

For example, you might do a little of everything that we discuss and although you'll have a broad succsess and have lots of cheques in your letterbox each month, you might not make as much as you would if you concentrated on a particular area.

Earlier we recommended that you concentrate on prodcuts that you're interested in, this is where you need to make up your mind on the busines model you choose. We don't have any particular instrest in Scuba diving but we sure make money out of our scuba website. The same goes for our Town and Country, Country and Outdoors and sporting websites.

We chose this method because it creates a passive, ongoing and broad approach to affiliate marketing but this approach is often dispised by 'professional' online business people as being unprofessional. These people also dispise the idea of reprodcing books that are in the public domain but we proved it worked with our book 'Acres of Diamonds'.

A third approach is a combination of both, sure you can invest time and resources into products and topics that you passionate about but if you're an investor buying shares you don't have to have a passion about oil to invest in oil shares. You can simply buy shares in oil to diversify your portfolio and in the same way you don't have to be passionate about a product or industry to make make money from it, but passion about learning methods of making a passive income will increase the methods that will produce that income for you.

Each product that you request to sell through Click Bank has an approval process as each supplier has their own criteria for the type of affiliate partners they wish to associate their brand with. Once approved, you'll receive an email and you can generate your own unique code for that product.

The Click Bank Website can provide you with tools to build your own website, we recommended Webnode simply because it's free and using free tools is a great way to learn.

There are two main ways you can look for products: you can search on particular keywords or sales statistics, or browse through product categories and sub-categories.

If you're not sure exactly what types of products to promote, choosing a general category can be a good place to start.

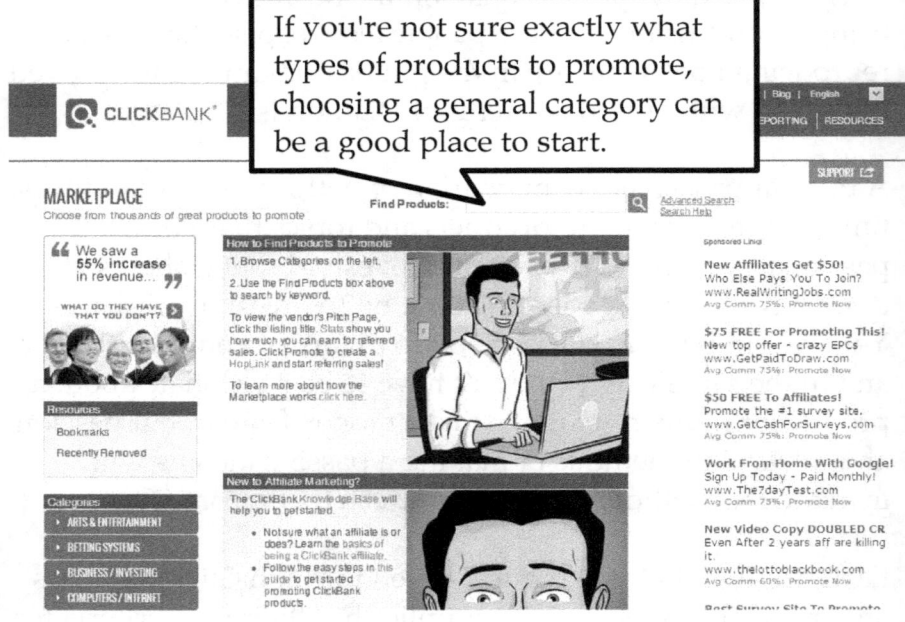

Let's look at some examples.

Cure For Tinnitus - Help People Stop The Ringing In Their Ears.

Super High Conversion Rates - Get Ready To Earn Money And Profit Big! Amazing Affiliate Support. More Affiliate Information Here: Http://www.curefortinnitus.com/affiliates

Avg $/sale

$20.60

Add To Favorites

Vendor Spotlight

Stats: Initial $/sale: $20.60 | Avg %/sale: 70.0% | Avg Rebill Total: $0.00 | Avg %/rebill: 0.0% | Grav: 5.28
Cat: Health & Fitness : Remedies

My Stats:

This product shows the average sale price is $20.60 and the commission is 70%

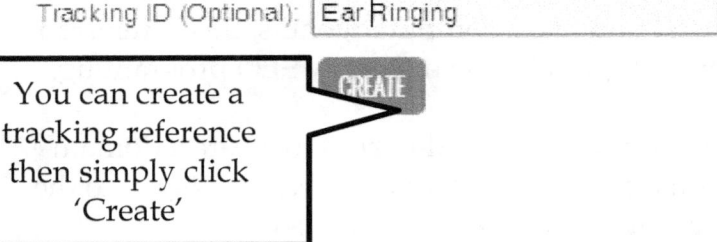

Tracking ID (Optional): Ear Ringing

CREATE

You can create a tracking reference then simply click 'Create'

This will open a new page where you simply copy the code in the same way we did with both AdSense and the Amazon program.

You can use this code (hop link) on your website or you can embed it in the text of your Blog. Pages 26 to 28 show you exactly how to do this.

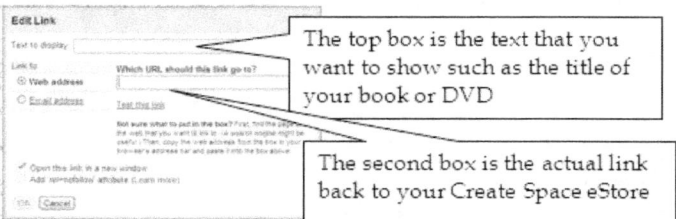

We also touched on the idea of Domain forwarding where you don't even need a website. The idea is to take advantage of the search engine process and key words.

Google Adwords key word tool – you'll need to be using Google Chrome or equivalent. The Key word tool can give you some ideas but some common sense and thought around what words people might use when they're searching will get you started.

If you want to sound like a computer genius, this is referred to as Search Engine Optimization or simply SEO programing.

Let's use GoDaddy **www.godaddy.com** to create a domain (this'll cost you a couple of dollars). But before you go to the Go Daddy website you can go to Fat Wallet **www.fatwallet.com** for a discount code that can be used when purchasing a Domain name.

When you have purchased a domain name you can forward that domain to any other website, Blog or even an Affiliate or your own link back to your Create Space eStore!

To do this through GoDaddy, log into your account and click on the domain name you have purchased.
This will bring up the control panel for that domain name.

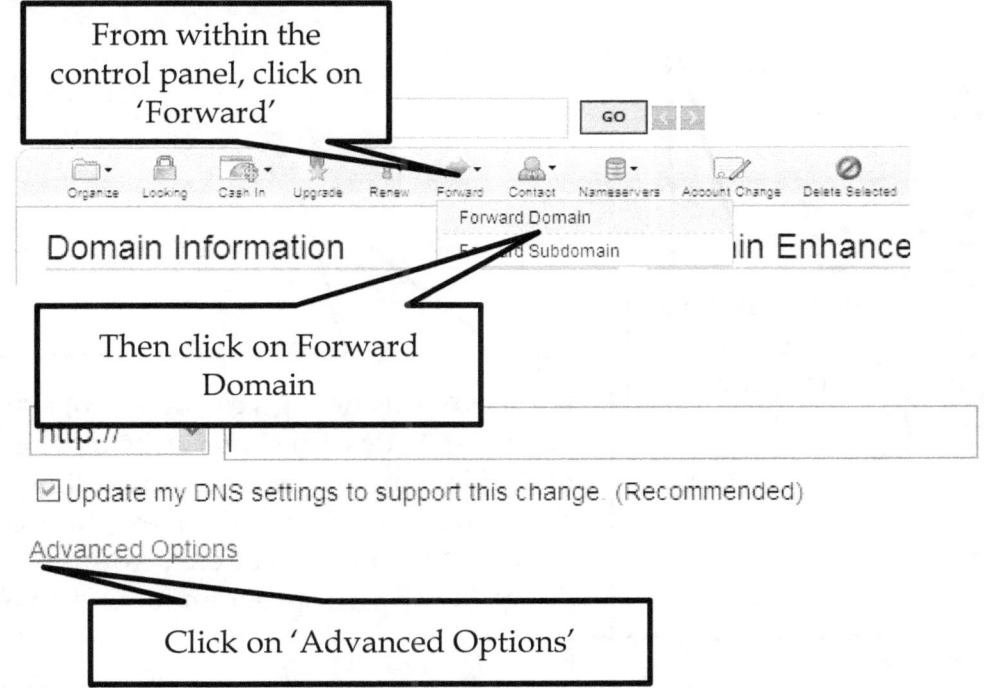

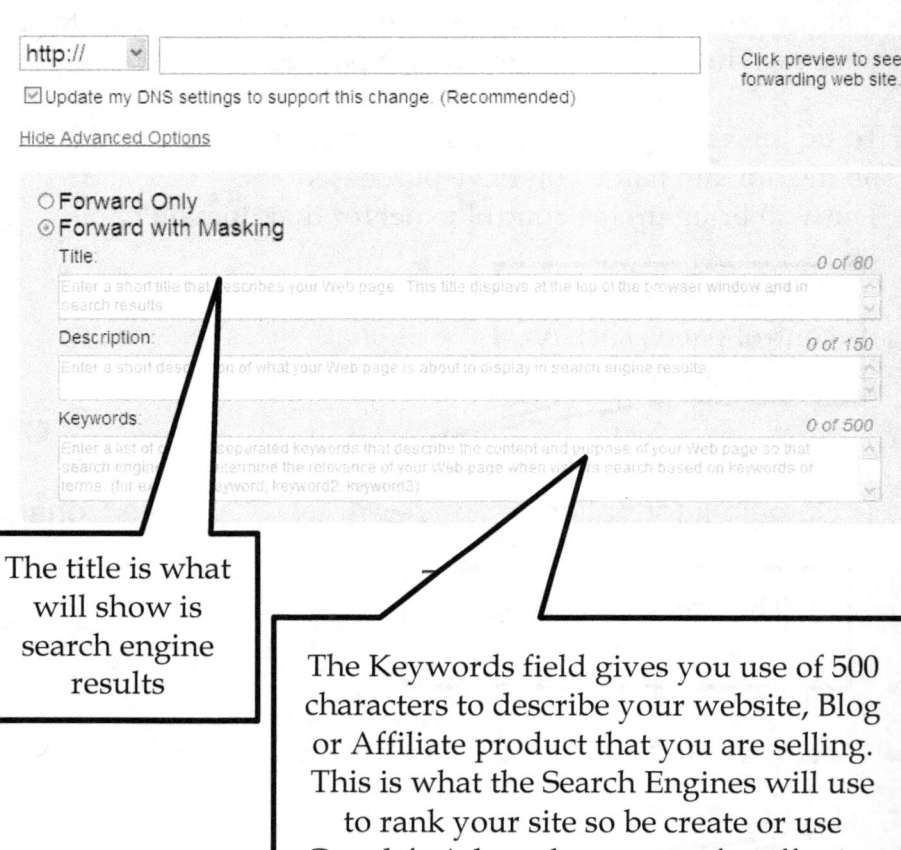

The title is what will show is search engine results

The Keywords field gives you use of 500 characters to describe your website, Blog or Affiliate product that you are selling. This is what the Search Engines will use to rank your site so be create or use Google's Adwords program for effective selections

Now you're an SEO genius!

Most Domain providers will allow you to 'Forward Domain'. Make sure you include the full link (or hoplink) that you use. The process can be used to create keywords that will be found by search engines to promote your own material (direct it to your blog, website or Create Space eStore) or you can forward it to an affiliate site. For example, you could create a non-specific sporting domain and forward it to through your Amazon link to 'sports' in Amazon or you could choose one product from your Click Bank account and promote it through simple Domain Forwarding.

Again, you'll need to decide on your own business model, most 'experts' say to be specific and concentrate on one product and to be the authority through blogs, websites, facebook, email, twitter and so on however, we're not experts on Scuba Diving but our Scuba website (and our other sites) make us ongoing passive income without original content or the care usually required in any other business.

The point we're making is that there are really no rules as to how you run your business. You can spend time being the expert in a particular field and concentrate on products, links and advertisments that are unique to that industry or you can spread yourself out to try and cover more bases through systems.

The same is true for both Primary and Secondary Income Producers, you can spend time creating original content for Primary Income producers such as Create Space, Café Press, iStock Photo, Kindle and e-Junkie (more on e-Junkie later) or you can concentrate on the Secondary income producers such as Google AdSense, Click Bank, Commission Junction and Amazon Affiliate programs.

The best model is what you are comfortable with while you're learning but a combination of both Primary and Secondary incomes with links between each other will create a compounding income for you.

Now you can see how the model works with time and work being spent *on* it instead of *in* it.

We mentioned using 'get Friday' and 'Fivver' to help by outsourcing your requirments for original content but you might still be asking yourself "What subject do I start with?" Layne and Staci wrote their book '50 Ways that People Make Extra Money for additional Income' by interviewing people who were already their clients.

They then began interviewing people for their CD series with a broad approach instead of a niche approach by simply interviewing people who were succseful in buisness. The people they interviewed at first were from manufacturing, financial services, taxation and even politics but as they had more seccess with sales, they realised it was the financial planning interviews that were selling the best so they made every two out of three interviews with a financial planning. It was after this that they were sponcered by an aggregation company to provide advertisments between each inerview and this cash injection allowed them to outsourse the interviews to provide international content.

What you do for a living might be a good start if you are stuck for ideas. If you're a Land Consultant, you could make a guide on how to subdivide land, if you're a Health Care professional you could suggest ideas to assist with managing everything from pain to making the house more practical for the person in care. If you enjoy gardening or organic vegetables, you could show people how to do it.

There are always people around you who would be happy to help, if you have an idea but not the expertise then ask somebody who does have the expertise and they may be happy to let you interview them, take photos and give you step by step instructions on how to fix that problem, get that job or build that bridge.

You can look at hobbies, business, careers, religion, facts, fiction, history, pets, families, transport, manufacturing, health, sports or fashion but remember it has to be helpful, informative or entertaining if it's going to make you money.

Of course, you can also make money indirectly by publishing material on behalf of another person. Now that you know how, you can upload that book, DVD or CD and publish it on behalf of those people or are not prepared to do the work you've just done to learn how to use Create Space, Blogger, You Tube and Amazon.

You can create a newsletter for someone who is too lazy to work out how to create links that sell products. You could take on the job of sending out emails as Craig does and promote products from his Amazon Affiliates program. You now have the knowledge to implement income producers into your everyday life!

Success Tip!

Think outside of the square, be different!

To this point we have covered methods of creating an online income with the criteria of;
 1.) No ongoing cost other than the registration of a domain name
 2.) No ongoing work to make the income truly passive and
 3.) No risk associated with the content we produced.
If these three criteria were to be applied to any other business model the prospect would be unrealistic but you have now seen that not only is it possible, it's by far the best way to run a business.

We also covered three different methods of creating an income being;
 1.) Original, physical content that can be sold as a book, DVD, CD or MP3 through Create Space and Lulu, an eBook through Kindle and even artwork for mugs, T-shirts and phone holders through Café Press and iStock Photo as Primary Income.
 2.) Affiliate income by specifically recommending products through suppliers such as Amazon, Click Bank and Commission Junction who pay you a commission for referring people to their products as Secondary Income and,
 3.) Advertising by utilising services from suppliers such as AdSense and Kontera (**http://kontera.com/**) who pay you a commission 'per click' with either or both text and picture advertising as 'Spin off' income through our Blog and You Tube.

In stage five we'll dig deeper into primary income as an advanced module but before we do its best that you familiarize yourself with the concepts, processes and websites that we used that don't cost you anything.

When creating your primary income, a "how-to" book or DVD is a great place to start because it's easy to promote and sell through the channels we've discussed. We've deliberately used methods of promoting your material that doesn't cost anything. It's fine to pay for advertising through providers such as Google once you have an understanding of how it works but you can have great success by using those same search words in the body and text of your website and blog without paying for them, so create your income first and once its producing an ongoing income stream you can then pay if you want to for advertising.

An easy place to start is with the knowledge or information that you already have. This can be your hobby, your profession or an interest. You may think that what you have is common knowledge but how did you get it?

You might be a keen hunter, a baker, or teacher but how did you obtain that knowledge and how long did it take you? If somebody read Layne and Staci's book "50 Ways that People make Extra Money for Additional Income" and decided to make some money by being a bounty hunter as Brian did, then where would they start. Brian grew up on a farm and he might suppose that everybody knows how to whistle in foxes and track with a spotlight but he learned those skills over years with his dad and brothers so if he made a DVD that could save somebody a year or two of trial and error, would that represent value for money? Of course it would.

You can also interview people or use services such as 'Get Friday' or 'Fivver' to compile the information that you want to publish as a way of getting started.

If you know you have great information to share but are not sure how it might be perceived 'professionally' then you might consider using a pseudonym.

Layne published his first book under his real name and although he was making money from it, he also noticed that his peers and manager at work were laughing about it behind his back and making remarks about what made him the expert in his field. Layne could have been discouraged by what turned out to be jealousy but instead he created a pseudonym or stage name that he published his blog and books under until he was established enough to use his real name again. Earlier we mentioned the importance of getting around like minded people and if the people you work with are not on your 'channel' then using a pseudonym or stage name might be a good idea, In the same way if you're a professional and concerned that publishing information based on your experience and knowledge might trigger the "Tall Poppy" in your work place then a stage name would be a wise choice.

The first thing to do now is "get started". You'll make mistakes along the way and that's all part of the learning experience, it's also the beauty of digital media because you can simply fix a mistake and upload it again.

Choose what media to use for your delivery, if you are going to put together a how-to manual on fighting and grappling techniques then a DVD might be better than a book. Most computers have some basic editing functions that are more than enough to get you started. Otherwise you could do a series of photos and make a book or even a slideshow with photos and on-screen instructions.

Set yourself goals that include a planned break down of the process. This might be a 10 day program to create your first website using Webnode, GoDaddy or Smartyhost or it might be to set up your first blog using Blogger or WordPress but get started.

By this stage you'll have the knowhow to build many more than just ten passive income streams online. You'll understand the concept of multiplying or compounding that income by creating links such as a blog that feeds to your website or Create Space eStore with the blog itself creating an income through AdSense advertising.

The ideas you've learned can be implemented on their own such as our Scuba Apparatus website that is nothing more than Amazon Affiliate pages, a couple of Click Bank ads and AdSense advertising or you can weave what you've learned into your daily life using tools you already have such as email, Facebook, newsletters and of course your current website if you have one or simply in your email signature.

Make sure you have approval from those concerned if you don't have direct ownership of the media. It's a bit more than just cheeky to insert an ad to a newsletter if you down that newsletter! When Layne and Staci were interviewing Craig for their book he said the first thing he did was get written authority to recommend products before putting his link into the newsletter, he also said he earns $500 to $600 a week from his one ad in each weekly newsletter!

Stage Five

The next level is a step up to sell your product as an affiliate marketer. We'll start with the Click Bank program where you share revenue with other people who also want to promote your product.

We recommend that you establish a good understanding of the previous stages before you invest both time and money with sales services such as Click bank.
In the same way, using search words to rank your own website instead of buying words or ranking programs are all you'll need until you get to the level of passive income where you don't mind investing some of it back into your online business model.

The Click bank system recommends a three stage approach where you have a first level product such as an ebook that you sell for a low price or even for free in exchange for the persons email address. You can market to that person via direct email to promote a secondary product at a higher price or even an ongoing monthly subscription.
To sell to the same customer over and over you would most likely have to be in a niche or specialized market. You could do this by providing ongoing training or support, by restricted 'member only' access to your website or simply by subscription to a monthly newsletter.

The affiliate program can provide a level of 'lead capture' for the initial contact or 'front end'; this would be your low end product offering that you will also share revenue with the affiliate marketer who referred the sale. It is then up to you to sell a compelling reason for that person to sign up for the more expensive 'back end' product, ongoing subscription or access to your video training library as a continuity program that provides you with regular and predictable income. This is where your business will require more work but the rewards can be huge.

This approach takes more to set up and maintain but allows you to step your clients up from a basic newsletter to a paid and in depth newsletter.
It allows you to step them up from a basic podcast to a full series. You can use webinar tools such as 'Go to Meeting' (**www.gotomeeting.com.au**) to host regular meetings and coaching courses.
The idea is to start with an initial lead and give the person something small in exchange for their email address to which you can pitch an ongoing product offering.

We've already covered the types of media you can use to capture your "how-to" information being written text, voice or video. People will pay to learn from someone how has been there and done that to save themselves time and money.

If you're still not sure where to start, you could try Squidoo (**http://www.squidoo.com/**) where you can write simple ideas, recipes or stories. kind of like a blog where Squidoo then runs their own ads and affiliate programs as a co-op and pays you a 50% share.

Trade shows by providers of affiliate and marketing programs can help you to meet other people with similar interests but the best way to get started is to dive in and give it a go.

E Junkie (**http://www.e-junkie.com/**) is an online tool to help you sell downloads as well as physical content, it's basically a shopping cart that you can merge with your website or you can use it as an affiliate program in a similar way to Click Bank.

http://www.crazyegg.com/ can help you track what buttons people 'favor' on your site to help you add more of what's being used and less of what's not. Crazy Egg can show you where people click on your site and how far down they scroll to help you determine what people are reading on your site and where those visitors have come from.

Get started, have fun and enjoy the process of creating many passive online income streams.

Covenant Land P/L -

P.O. Box 1047, Ringwood, Victoria, Australia. 3134

info@covland.com

www.ingramcontent.com/pod-product-compliance
Lightning Source LLC
Chambersburg PA
CBHW071624170526
45166CB00003B/1189